MARKETING STEAMY ROMANCE

KILBY BLADES

LUXE PRESS

Published by Luxe Press 2018

For permission requests and other inquiries, the publisher can be reached at: info@luxepress.net

Print Edition ISBN 10: 0-9991532-1-8

Print Edition ISBN 13: 978-0-9991532-1-5

Cover by Cover Me Darling: www.covermedarling.com

Editing by Plotbunny: www.plotbunnyediting.com

To my wicked-penned, big-pimping, pro-author friends. Your collaboration and fellowship inspires me.

INTRODUCTION

Excellent manuals have been written about mainstream book marketing. The more PG-rated your subject-matter, the greater your ability to use everything from big ad channels to ingenious little tactics to earn new readers. I've heard a lot of cute advice, like to leave a copy in every Starbuck's and waiting room you visit, or to hijack shelf space in a retail bookstore by smuggling your book inside and placing it on a display. That may be fine for a cozy mystery or a how-to book about growing orchids. But it's not fine for books that are rated NC-17.

In my debut novel, *Snapdragon*, the sexy times start happening around page 18. How well do you think it would turn out if a teenager picked it up in the waiting room of a doctor's office? Probably pretty well for the teenager. But if his mom caught on to why he'd lost interest in his phone and had covered his lap with his sweater, things wouldn't turn out as well for me.

Keeping material away from audiences who shouldn't—or just plain don't want to—be exposed to explicit fiction is at the heart of why steamy romance can't be advertised anywhere or in any way it darn-well pleases. The big ad platforms are a little like 7-11 was in the eighties with its porn magazines—if you're looking for the sexy stuff, it's there. But it's tucked away in a discreet corner behind the counter, with opaque plastic shields obscuring racy covers from easily-offended eyes. It's the gatekeeper's job (the cashier) to make sure it doesn't fall into the wrong hands.

The Amazons and Facebooks of the world are today's gatekeepers. Not just those two, but any retailer or website publisher that actively curates and standardizes its content. It's not that they won't allow material with adult themes—it's that they tightly control the visibility of these materials. This book is about how to market content that retailers and website publishers don't think that everybody should be allowed to see.

What This Book Isn't

If you're looking for book advertising basics, this probably isn't your book. There is a tremendous body of knowledge with a general focus on advertising for authors, and on my web site, I post reviews for books and courses I like. Though, in this book, you'll find chapters on newsletters, paid advertising, book covers, and other marketing topics, they are not written with universal advice in mind. Instead, they give highly specific advice around how to craft your marketing assets and get the most out of common channels if your books are steamy.

What is Steamy Romance?

Throughout this book, I'll use terms like "steamy romance" and "erotic fiction" interchangeably to broadly refer to the category in question. Yet, much of the advice you'll find is relevant to any sort of prohibited literature. I realize that not all sexually explicit books contain romance, and that books are flagged for all sorts of "unsuitable" content—not just those featuring erotic themes. This book has insights for any author writing material that shows readers what happens behind closed doors and deals with all brands of socially-questioned taboo.

Let's talk, for a minute, about the difference between mature themes and explicit content. Millions of books allude to things adults do to or with one-another without ever letting the reader see them play out on the page. Implied sex is different from graphic sex. A book that tells readers that a minor has sex with an adult is different from one that shows it. And again, it's not just sex—it's any taboo act that falls outside of suitability guidelines. The more vague a book is about sexy or taboo subjects, the less likely it is to violate a content rule.

With that said, graphic sex and sexual taboos in particular seem to be under fire—especially sex in books that self-identify as romance and erotica. My own books—which are tasteful, well-written, well-rated, and pretty vanilla as far as sex goes—have been rejected from every major advertising platform. I won't go so far as to call it common, but it is frequent that I hear from authors whose sexually explicit books have been pulled from retailer listings altogether. My own firsthand challenges and the challenges of those close to me were what prompted me to write this book.

Getting Real About What Authors of Erotic Romance Face

At times, the risks and challenges in this book may seem overstated or alarmist. Surely, all of us can think of erotic romance authors who are listing books and advertising wherever they want. I can't underscore enough how often book sales and string-pulling create leniency for those who don't seem to be following the rules. If you're selling a lot of books, spending big dollars with mainstream advertisers, or have the weight of a major publishing house behind you, gatekeepers are inclined to look the other way. Double standards like these mean less favorable outcomes for smaller-time authors with little bargaining power.

If this seems like madness, it is. Publishing has always harbored sacred cows. Beyond placing restrictions on sexually explicit content, most retailer guidelines outright prohibit the sale of books containing persistent, graphic and violent acts. Yet, works like *American Psycho* by Bret Easton Ellis, *Naked Lunch* by William Burroughs, and *The Road* by Cormack McCarthy are widely available for purchase. *Naked Lunch*, in particular, has scores of complaints about the graphic content in the one- and two-star Amazon ratings and only 59% positive reviews. Yet, people still buy it, and it's even listed on Amazon under Classics. More importantly, it still ranks. As of the writing of this book it was #32 in its category even though it was first published nearly sixty years ago, in 1959. Because it sells, it will never be taken down.

Beyond selling as many ads or books as possible, gatekeepers have other incentives. Their goal isn't to be fair and circumspect around what questionable content is approved—its to be conservative if necessary in protecting their own reputations. Facebook saw a huge backlash in 2017 over ad scams, fake news and trashy ad content. Their response has been to crack down. In May of that year, they issued a statement that was covered by CNET, Business Insider, and ABC Online confirming a policy change. In the absence of processes that do a good job of sorting out the trash, they'll err on the side of keeping out ten things that deserve a pass so they don't suffer the fallout from letting one wrong thing through.

And, about process...deficiencies here are also to blame for double-standards. If you think a fair, intelligent, well-paid human who is qualified to do his job is sitting in a comfy office somewhere making good decisions about what is acceptable, you're wrong. Gatekeepers employ some combination of robots and humans to screen tens of millions of advertisements for prohibited content. Amazon is pulling double-duty, screening not only advertisements but also books. The human reviewing your asset —if your asset even makes it to a human—has neither the time and possibly not the expertise to understand where or whether your ad or book belongs. The book you slaved over may get less than a minute of focused, tender loving care.

This is unfair and disappointing, especially when you see that the door has been opened to other authors whose materials have similar attributes, only to find your own door closed. Some of it is luck. The human who rejected your ad may be more heavy-handed than his colleague who would have let the same ad through. Technically, *all* of the listings and ads we see for steamy books are in violation of retailer and advertising guidelines. Their legalese is written in ways that define mature content broadly and give gatekeepers authority to restrict whatever content they want. If you have the time, money and stamina to pull together a class action lawsuit to fight sweeping enforcement discrepancies, be my guest. For individual appeals, the law is not on your side.

I could go deeper on this topic, and tell you to thank our puritanical roots for this war on sex (or, more accurately, this tolerance for books portraying patriarchal sexual violence over those portraying female sexual pleasure). But if I get on my soapbox about that, you'll never hear my advertising advice. So let's jump into that, shall we? After all, that's what you've come here for.

How The Book Is Organized

You'll get the most out of this book if you read it sequentially. I don't like to be repetitive, so I won't go overboard on reiterating key ideas. For example, I'll use the book cover chapter to describe what kind of art may fail to be approved. Three chapters later, when I write about creating ads, I'll assume you're familiar with background I gave earlier on how to choose approvable art.

If you're comfortable with the basics and there's a topic that interests you, by all means, skip right to it. Know that you may still find value in skimming through topics you're familiar with if you want to read about some hacks and pro tips I've learned. Overall, the book has been designed to be easy to follow and to respect your time as an author or advertising pro. I'm glad you're allocating time toward building skills around marketing steamy romance, but I know you'd rather be doing the hands-on work of promoting or writing.

The first section, *Avoiding Land Mines*, is focused on how to plan and develop your core marketing assets according to your advertising intention. An introductory chapter presents the two distinct paths authors must choose between in today's marketplace. One path is to tone your assets down in order to conform to mainstream ad platform guidelines. The other is to focus your efforts on channels more friendly to steamy romance. Subsequent chapters in this section feature differentiated advice, supplying strategies for mainstreamers as well as purists who want creative flexibility. Topics include:

- Deciding whether to advertise on major platforms
- Strategizing book covers, titles and blurbs
- Required and optional disclosures
- Creating ads and video trailers

Section two, called *Going Off-Script*, introduces tactics that can be used by authors whose marketing decisions will shut them out of mainstream advertising schemes. If your book cover features models who are nearly naked, you drop an f-bomb in the blurb, and you've categorized it as erotica, this is the section for you. Not all authors are willing to tone down their marketing assets. There's nothing wrong with that. This section talks about other paths that are wise for purists and mainstreamers alike. I'll talk about:

- Building an e-mail list and using newsletters
- How to get the most out of your web site

- Paid advertisements on book marketing web sites and blogs that sell advertising
- Awards and contests
- Influencer tactics (e.g. PR, PAs, unpaid bloggers)
- Unique and creative opportunities

Section three, called *Covering Your Ass* is about mitigating risk, regardless of your book's marketing plan. It discusses common situations you may come across after your assets are in place and has a meaty final chapter that discusses being smart about budgeting, setting ad performance expectations and measuring advertising results. I'll cover:

- Dealing with bans and blocks
- Dealing with reviews from disgruntled readers
- Covering your financial ass and not going broke with paid advertising
- Getting your house in order

And there's more beyond the advice presented in the book itself. A supporting website, www.marketingsteamyromance.com features resource lists and reviews of my favorite tools. The environment is ever-changing, and joining my newsletter will help you stay abreast of issues impacting the marketing landscape.

PART ONE

AVOIDING
LAND MINES

CHAPTER ONE

THE MOST IMPORTANT DECISION

First things first. The *Avoiding Land Mines* section is about tradeoffs authors have to make depending on where they plan to advertise. Before you take a word of my advice, you have a big decision to make: is advertising on the major platforms right for you? By major platforms, I mean media giants with vast, well-developed and automated ad networks. You will see me mention Amazon and Facebook ads explicitly, but for other huge platforms such as Twitter, and even Google (particularly the display network), this distinction also applies. Major platforms have stringent rules that present challenges to any author of explicit content.

Though they offer unparalleled reach, major platforms are more conservative than all other channels presented in this book. Including them in your plan requires a willingness to craft your core marketing assets—from covers, to blurbs, to titles—to conform to what they're willing to let through. Regardless of the stories you tell on the page, the way you position your books matters. I don't want you flushing your money down the toilet developing assets that will never make it through approval processes. Conversely, I don't want you to worry about some of the warnings discussed in this section if major platform advertising is something you shouldn't pursue.

Let's say you write an office romance. If you call it *Boss Lady* and put a fully-clothed woman in a suit on the cover, then place it in the New Adult and College category on Amazon, advertising on major platforms is unlikely to be a problem. On the other hand, if you call it *Screwed by My Supervisor*, put a scantily-clad couple making out on the cover, and classify it as Erotica, a paid promotion on the same platforms will never be approved. The advice contained in this section is designed to get you clear on your strategy, and to show you how to transcend strict guidelines using my tips, tricks and hacks.

Before we fully dive into this topic, I want to make it clear what I'm advocating for, and to talk about the difference between making conscious decisions about brand positioning and misleading others by gaming the system. Please don't create covers, blurbs, or choose categories that mislead readers about what they will find in your book. Authors who do this contribute to why some retailers' policies toward authors have become so unforgiving.

ARE MAJOR PLATFORMS FOR YOU?

Now, let's talk about who stands to benefit most from major platform advertising. Keeping options open to advertise as widely as possible will matter to some authors more than others. The big platforms have access to millions of users who they know a lot about thanks to creepy practices that retain and analyze a wealth of behavioral data. In a March 2017 article, *The Guardian* called this "surveillance capitalism" and reported that Facebook holds 98 data points on every user. Not only do major platforms have the reach to place your ads in front of hundreds of thousands of targeted prospects—they can serve up a steady flow of new readers if you target users and manage campaigns effectively.

To give you a sense for the horsepower behind some of these

tools, I'll start with Facebook. Its ad product offers endless opportunities to target by interests, and to further narrow by demographic, psychographic and location. Because their real currency is understanding what's important to users, it's easy to use their ad system to hone in directly on pre-sorted audiences, including ones related to erotic romance. Literally, if you create a Facebook ad and type in terms such as "erotic romance", "romance novels," and "erotica" when you're in the targeting interface, established user audiences will pop up.

If you want to get fancy, you can target ads to users who follow specific pages and who like specific authors. If you want to get even fancier, watch how your campaigns are performing and further narrow your targeting to those who fit the highest engagement behaviors. There are many other advanced features. My favorite is one called Custom Audiences, which lets you import e-mail addresses, use pixel data, and work in other integrations to laser-focus your reach to certain users. Say you have an e-mail list of 10,000 subscribers—you can upload that list to Facebook's ad tool and run ads that only serve to e-mail addresses among that list that match to a Facebook profile.

It's difficult to convey the sheer scope of what you can do on Facebook, and it's important to know that its capabilities are only growing. The ad formats you may be most familiar with are still image and video ads that appear in your newsfeed and on the right sidebar of a desktop page. Newer formats include Facebook Messenger ads that target users' chat inboxes, Instagram ads, mobile takeovers, and even ads that pop up a signup form that users can fill out without leaving their Facebook feed.

Amazon has other capabilities. There, you can target ads to specific keywords, or even advertise against specific books. Do you remember those old commercials for Designer Impostor Body Sprays? They featured aerosol perfumes that smelled like designer fragrances. The sultry female voice-over informed you that if you liked Giorgio, you'd love Primo, their copycat scent. I'm not calling you a copycat. But if you're aware of other books that are similar to yours in writing quality, genre and trope, Amazon Marketing Services(AMS) lets you laser in on readers who may be open to your book.

You'd have to be kind of an idiot to not at least *want* to use the mainstream ad networks. The problem is, they're not always friendly to erotic romance. Your ads have a better chance of being approved if your art and descriptions are relatively tame, and if you haven't done something along the way to flag your content as adult.

If you're adamant about signaling how hot and dirty your book is, your decision is already made. For you, becoming a mainstreamer is out. But if ad capabilities such as this sound too good to pass up, you may have to sacrifice creative vision (not to mention the chance to dazzle the set of readers who want the steam flaunted in their face) and fall in line.

If you're on the fence, or just want more variables to consider, authors in the following situations may have extra incentives to go the mainstream route:

- AUTHORS WHOSE WRITING ISN'T REALLY THAT STEAMY. I get it. Reading your books would make your grandmother blush. Or cross herself. Or march outside to get a switch and give you a good whooping. But there's a difference between teapot and locomotive steam. Does your book just show people doing things that everybody does? Or does it portray extreme detail or show an alternative lifestyle? The point is, don't close doors that might otherwise be open to you by over-signaling the heat level of your book.
- AUTHORS WHO HAVE ALREADY EXHAUSTED OTHER TACTICS. If you've already done other smart things to reach readers and you feel like you've hit a plateau, major platforms may offer the additional reach you need. If you have a mailing list and social media

followers already, Facebook in particular will allow you to exclude audiences like this and show ads only to those who haven't been exposed to you and your books. Facebook also gives you greater control of making sure the same people aren't seeing your ads over and over—this is called frequency capping. It's more insurance that you're exposing your ads only to new audiences.

- AUTHORS WHO WANT ONE-STOP SHOPPING. Not every author likes the hustle. And, come on— maintaining a website, sending out newsletters, and not making enemies on social media is a lot of work. If you're not into the idea of building your personal brand, major platforms let you stay in your cave and simply put your campaigns to work. I'm not saying it's a great idea to put all your eggs in one basket, but only you can decide how much you're willing to do. If you decide you can do only one thing to funnel in new readers, work the major platforms and invest in doing it well.

- AUTHORS WHO WANT TO BETTER-UNDERSTAND THEIR AUDIENCES. Part two presents a number of tactics that are effective at selling books but that give no information about who is engaging. As an example, the last single-day promo I did on a site called BargainBooksy sold more than 80 books. Do you know what I learned about the people who bought? Nothing. Tactics like these just drive sales—they don't get you insights, and there's a value to knowing what's working. Looking at performance on data-driven campaign platforms will tell you a lot about who is buying your books. Major platforms also make it easier for you to run good tests on ad messages that may or may not be working.

WHEN TO AVOID MAJOR PLATFORM ADVERTISING

You've heard the case for what major platforms offer. Let's talk now about deal-breakers. The big one—in some ways, the only one—is creative integrity. If you want everyone to know how smoking hot your books are, there are scores of reasons to signal that. Readers don't care about caution. For a lot of them, the dirtier the cover and the description, the better. Many top-ranked authors are killing it with assets that are way too racy to advertise but just the perfect amount of racy for voracious, smut-loving readers. These authors aren't using major platforms at all.

So much of what will feel right for your library is personal. Compromising your vision is the design equivalent of writing to market. Maybe you don't care that reverse harem is trending right now—you just want to write what you like to write. The same is true for the external assets that will serve as signals for what's inside your book.

Don't get me wrong—I want you to step up your marketing game and multiply your sales, but not if you have to fight off a wave of nausea every time you look at your own books. So, if you hate the idea of compromise, and you doubly hate the idea of lining the pockets of companies that treat our genre as the red-headed stepchildren of publishing, take your fabulous ginger ass and look elsewhere to build your tribe. It's been my experience that authors with the most individuality and the strongest sense of themselves do just fine at building communities of adoring readers.

LOVE IS A BATTLEFIELD

Have you ever seen an episode of *Mad Men*? Advertising is a vicious business. And it takes a lot of people to get it right. At a traditional ad agency, you will find a creative department that develops art, a copy department that writes ads, a research department that understands target markets and campaign results, and a Don Draper type to lead the overall vision. We've come a long way since the ad agencies of the 1960s but digital advertising has the same bones. Marketing, like writing, is a skilled profession. People go to school to learn it and spend years honing their craft. If you're going to work with major platforms, you'd better have a plan for creating, targeting, measuring, and optimizing your ads.

This is harsh advice for most people to hear. Indeed, the major platforms seduce users into thinking that advertising will be easy. When Facebook suggests that you boost a post to reach several thousand more people, or when Amazon e-mails KDP authors pitches to advertise through AMS, make no mistake — they are marketing to you. *Of course* they want you to advertise — both companies make a lot of money from ad revenue. Facebook may not care if you fail, but I do. If you aren't in a position to make campaigns on major platforms successful, I don't want you to waste your money. Here are a few deal breakers that may disqualify you right off the bat. If any of these are true for you, think twice.

WHEN YOUR BUDGET IS RAZOR THIN. I don't care if you're the best digital marketer in the world, if you're broke, advertising a few dollars a week won't make a difference. Digital advertising only makes money when it can be optimized — but optimization requires data. You have to expose enough people and audiences to your ads before you can find a repeatable formula that works.

Most basic digital advertising is pay-per-click (PPC). That means you pay when somebody clicks on your ad. But only a small number of people who click, convert. A "conversion" is a sale, and a 10% conversion rate would be a strong early result. But, let's do the math. If 10% of people who click on your ad buy your book, that means that for every ten books you actually sell, you've had to pay for a hundred clicks. If clicks cost $0.25 apiece, you've just spent $25 to sell ten books.

This example points to two hard facts of advertising: first, that in order to move the needle on sales, you often have to spend at scale. If you were looking to sell forty more books a week, with these numbers, you would have to either spend $100 per week on advertising or optimize your campaigns in a way that brings your cost per click down and your conversion rate up. That leads to the second hard fact: your early attempts are likely to fail. You will blow some budget learning what works vs. what doesn't. If sales are your goal, and you want campaigns to be profitable, it is very difficult to succeed without an initial investment of at least several hundred dollars and very smart optimization to figure out a repeatable success formula.

WHEN YOU LACK THE SKILLS, OR THE TEAM, TO RUN EFFEC-TIVE CAMPAIGNS. I always shake my head when I hear overgen-eralized statements like "Amazon ads are a ripoff" or "Facebook ads don't work." They work for people who know how to make them work. Running digital campaigns is a skilled profession, just like writing books. People who get great marketing results are the ones who know their craft.

Finally, campaign quality matters. A 10% conversion rate is harder than you think to achieve. Your ad copy and creative, as well as how well you show on a retailer site have to be on point. Readers who click on ads and land on a retailer site will convert well only if they find a great cover, blurb and star rating. In other words, don't underestimate how much skill goes into running a campaign. You don't have to merely do it, you have to be able to do it well.

Mark Dawson is a marketer whose work I admire. He's developed a solid curriculum on book marketing for authors. It is a thoughtful, accurate introduction to digital marketing strategies for authors. Even the first of his modules, "Facebook Ads For Authors" is separated into video lessons that add up to more than

15 hours of instruction. And that's just Facebook. YouTube, Twitter, Amazon and other platforms are separate modules.

I'm not saying this to intimidate you. But I don't want to blow sunshine up your ass. Any schmuck can create a Facebook ad. But not many people can actually make it work. That doesn't mean you can't become great at it. But if you're not committed to that path of learning, or to hiring the right talent resource who knows what she's doing, forget it.

FINAL NOTE: THE HYBRID APPROACH

It's possible that you won't be able to use major platforms for ads intended to sell books. That doesn't mean you can't use them as a tool for other things. Even if your covers are too racy, you can use digital campaigns to drive e-mail list signups, page follows and other engagement that supports the overall marketing mix. On Amazon, authors can do giveaways that require prospective readers to follow their profiles. On Facebook, campaigns can work to get followers for nearly any purpose. As long as you don't use art that's too racy in the ads, you've got a shot at being approved and using these kinds of campaigns to aid other marketing goals.

If shaky campaign management skills are your issue, stay away from Facebook and consider skewing toward platforms that have fewer variables. For example, AMS is less complex in terms of targeting options and ad formats advertisers are given, and is therefore easier to use. Certain Google advertising products, such as those offered by YouTube, also have fewer variables. Mail services like MailChimp have watered down ad integrations that may be better for beginners, too.

CHAPTER TWO

BOOK COVERS, TITLES AND BLURBS

That old adage about not judging books by their covers is bullshit—we all know that covers sell books. A great cover is the most important investment an author can make in driving split-second interest. The cardinal rule of book cover design is to choose evocative, high-quality art that signals genre. A good steamy romance cover can send the fingers of even the strong of heart fluttering to their collarbones to clutch their pearls. Sometimes, capturing the reader with a cover that signals heat is exactly what is needed to sell a book.

But there are more than just readers to consider. Make your covers too sexy, and they might get banned by advertisers and social platforms (not to mention, serve as easy fruit for picking on by easily-offended readers). Make them too vague, and there's no guarantee the reader will pick up on genre and tropes. This chapter will help you hedge against creating covers you're in love with, only to have to deal with wrist-slapping from an important gatekeeper who doesn't love them back.

COVERS FOR LISTING VS. COVERS FOR ADVERTISING

I know what you're thinking about: all those covers that are dripping with sex, some of which have succeeded as bestsellers. Now, go through that list again and think about how many of them you actually saw advertised on a major platform like Amazon or Facebook. Better yet, go to Amazon right now and do a search for "Erotic Romance" (I just did it myself.) The book I see in the ad spot, *Uncovered* by Kathryn Taylor, doesn't even have humans on the cover. What it does have is a solid purple background and a simple visual scheme of white feathers falling through the air.

A search for "Steamy Romance" yielded an ad for three fantasy novels, their covers shown with men so muscular they barely appeared to be able to keep their shirts buttoned. What I didn't see advertised (and what you won't either) are covers that Amazon has deemed to be too explicit. It's not that you can't *list* a book with a sexy cover on a retailer web site — it's that, if the art is overtly sexy, listing (and not advertising) it is all you may be able to do.

Organic search results are a different story — by organic, I mean the unsponsored results that appear below the advertisements. Any listing can appear in organic results if a combination of categories, keywords and sales push it up to make it more visible. Somebody who searches for your author name will find you as part of these search results. But your desire to reach new readers may be hampered if you are shut out of advertising with the majors.

And that's just advertising. If your book contains material that is too taboo, the delicate sensibilities of retailers might not be able to stomach it, and there's a chance they won't let you list it at all. This chapter will show you land mines to avoid to minimize the risk that you'll be banned for either.

POLICIES (AND THEIR ARBITRARY ENFORCEMENT)

Officially, the Amazon Advertising Creative Acceptance Policy prohibits the advertisement of content that contains "overtly provocative imagery such as partial nudity or blatantly sexual prurient content". A different section about advertising on Amazon Kindle, Fire Tablet and Fire TV reiterates this, warning against the advertisement of "mature, sensitive, and controversial" material. The former deals with visual cues supplied by the cover, and the latter extends restrictions to the content contained within.

Facebook is much the same. It hosts an adult content page within its advertising policies that currently prohibits "1) nudity or implied nudity, even if artistic or educational in nature, 2) excessive visible skin or cleavage, even if not explicitly sexual in nature, and 3) images focused on individual body parts, such as abs, buttocks or chest, even if not explicitly sexual in nature." Anyone who reads or writes steamy romance knows that these policies, if carried out judiciously, would disqualify most novels listed in the erotic category and at least half of novels currently listed in any sub-genre of romance.

The second you check the box at the bottom of the form when you're setting up your account, and agree to the legalese that nobody bothers to read, you've been warned. If your cover is banned, the ad platform will never be obligated to reverse their decision. If you're an author with big sales, or if you're signed to a big publisher with a portfolio of important authors, you may get more leniency than the rest of us. What's useful to the average author is to know that these policies are enforced arbitrarily. It's smart to assume they'll apply to you.

I learned this the hard way. For my book, *Snapdragon*, I had a beautiful cover designed that showed only its namesake flower. But the closer I got to the release date, I got cold feet. From the cover alone, the genre was ambiguous. It looked more like a literary fiction cover than it did romance. As an unknown author,

I reasoned that signaling as vague as this might hurt me as I tried to recruit readers. So I changed the cover, to a couple kissing, naked from the waist-up. What it gained me was good genre signaling. What it cost me was the ability to advertise the book.

YOUR OPTIONS

Even with the risks I've mentioned, what you decide for your cover is still a choice. If you want every channel open to you, be conservative. If you want to focus on what you think your readers will respond to, flip major platforms the bird. The important thing is to go into your choice with eyes wide open. Be honest with yourself about what a risqué cover will cost you, and what doors might open by virtue of toning down the steam.

- OPTION 1: PLAY IT SAFE. Your first option is subtlety. I won't mention specific books because I don't want to single out individual authors or throw anyone under the bus. Suffice it to say that many clean-ish covers found on Facebook and Amazon ads lead readers to very dirty books. Look at books that are advertising under keywords for erotic sub-genres and the names of other steamy reads. You can tell pretty clearly from the reviews and the blurbs how sexy they are. Plenty of authors are wise to putting toned-down covers on not-toned-down books.
- OPTION 2: USE WHATEVER COVER YOU WANT. If you're not set on mainstreaming your advertising, go with whatever cover you want. One of my favorite covers is the first in the *Call Girls* series by Emma Jaye. It shows the very sexy curve of the breast of a well-endowed woman. Even without its racy title, the cover makes for no mistaking the sexual themes in the book. It's not so racy that Amazon won't list it—but it is too racy for advertising on big platforms. It's a

calculated decision that wins readers who will respond more readily to the sexy stuff. Covers like this can still be advertised through niche channels. If you take this approach, you'll have to heavy up on non-mainstream tactics. A wealth of advice on those awaits you in Part II.

- **OPTION 3: TAKE A CHANCE, BUT BE WILLING TO SWITCH.** A third option is to roll the dice on a cover that's borderline and see what happens. Create an ad that features the cover and you'll quickly learn whether it will be approved. On Facebook in particular, you can run a test before you even list your book. With this option, be ready for the decision. If you're dead-set on using major platforms for advertising, you might need to stomach going back to the drawing board and coming up with (not to mention paying for) a cover that can be approved.
- **ADVANCED STRATEGIES.** One good option is to take a hybrid approach: if you have a particular book or series that you want to use to funnel new readers into your library, err on the side of caution. Use a tame cover for this starter book and advertise it liberally. Once you've hooked readers, and are selling books by stepping readers through your library, it won't matter as much if you have racy covers on subsequent books.

COVER DESIGN RULES THAT AVOID RESTRICTIONS

If you've decided to play it safe—or at least somewhat safe—here are a few considerations. Being conservative here will maximize the chances that your cover gets through. Even the big publishers are wise to these distinctions, and you'll see that the covers of many huge authors are already conforming to these rules.

- **HUMANS VS. NOT-HUMANS.** You may have noticed that some of the raciest books don't feature humans at all. The cover of E.L. James' *Fifty Shades of Grey* is a silvery tie. Sylvia Day's *Bared To You* has cufflinks. Tara Sue Me's *The Submissive* has a diamond choker and her more recent book covers feature black backgrounds with vividly-colored flowers. Showing flowers and meaning sex is very Georgia O'Keefe. Luckily, a ton of readers understand that flowers mean vaginas and that the diamond necklace isn't a choker—it's a collar. More than ever, readers don't need to see humans practically having sex in the cover art to understand when the genre is steamy romance. No actual bodice-ripping or Fabio-esque cover models are required.

- **FLAUNTING MALE SEXUALITY VS. FEMALE SEXUALITY.** Yeah. I know. It's 2018. And female sexuality is still super-threatening. That's why covers that show a lot of skin—particularly a lot of female skin—are more likely to be rejected for advertising on big platforms. Even being cleared for listing on retailer sites with covers that push the envelope on images of women can be dicey. One author told me her cover was rejected by Amazon because it showed side-boob. It's not a mistake that covers with nearly-naked men are nearly ubiquitous today in the genre. This isn't the case because readers clamored to have women pushed off of covers. Rather, authors and publishers became savvy to the confines of the system. If your audience is hetero women, there are other reasons to put a man on the cover. These readers don't just fall in love with stories—they fall in love with heroes, a fact which, in itself, can make showing a sexy man wise. However, if a strong heroine is at the center of your book and you're trying to attract readers who are actively seeking that quality, a fully-clothed badass woman, might be a better choice.

- SEXY VS. NON-SEXY BODY PARTS. One of my favorite book covers is *Wallbanger* by Alice Clayton. In this cover, we are shown the back of a fully-clothed man standing in front of an also-clothed woman. Though her body is covered by his, we can see they are facing one another. Her legs wrap around his midsection and cross at the ankles, and her arms are around his neck. Apart from the woman's hands, we see no bare skin. She is wearing shoes and her legs are stockinged. From beyond the man's hips we see evidence that she's wearing a skirt. Even with the trick of having them fully clothed, this cover gives the intended impression: that the couple is doing something very naughty, and that the reader can count on a steamy book. I'll be honest and say that I don't know whether her publishers advertised this book on any of the mainstream platforms, and even if they did, having a big publisher to tip the scales gives plenty of authors space to break the rules. The point here is that it's possible for a cover to be very sexy—even without breasts or bulges, six-pack abs or excessive skin. Even without ecstatic facial expressions or other typical signals, creative solutions can find heat levels perfectly-conveyed.

A final rule about cover design is to avoid playing it so safe that your cover gets lost in the shuffle. Check out Sarah Stein, who wrote a book called *Her Will*. It's about a southern domme named Jolene and her cover is a black and purple leather whip on a bed of red satin fabric. What I love about this cover is that it signals the genre without looking like every other BDSM novel. Without using scantily-clad models, the cover art supplies the perfect signal to the indoctrinated reader. Another example,

Caught Up in Raine by L.G. O'Connor shows a hot, shirtless male model like so many other novels right now. By verbal description, it sounds like it's pretty standard. But, go check it out—the model's look is so distinctive, and the rest of the styling is so high-quality that, even with a widely-used format, it really stands out.

TITLES MATTER TOO

Even if your cover isn't suggestive, your title might be. This can be grounds for ad disapprovals. I don't care if you have beagle puppies in scrubs as your cover art. If the title of your book is *Naughty Nurse Threesomes*, you're on rocky ground. Nearly anything goes on Amazon in terms of titles I've seen allowed for standard book listings. Enforcement of what's allowed for advertising purposes remains riddled with serious double standards. In other words, just because you see ads for other books with racy keywords as part of your research doesn't mean that your title with equally racy (if not identical) phrases will go through. Final decisions are at their discretion, and they can point to their policies which, in writing, would make a title like *Naughty Nurse Threesomes* against the rules.

As you think through tradeoffs around title choice, here are things to consider:

- KEYWORD SEARCHABILITY. Many readers search for books based on micro-genres. It's no coincidence that authors include in their titles words like "millionaire", "billionaire" and "CEO" when such keywords align to tropes. It's harder for readers to find books containing tropes they like if the title does nothing to signal them. Including the name of a risqué trope as part of your title (such as "orgy" or "swingers" will limit ad opportunities for your book).
- VAGUE AND ARBITRARY TITLES. The opposite of

keyword-infused titles are those that are vague and arbitrary. My books fall into this camp: the sequel to *Snapdragon* is called *Chrysalis*. My first novella, *The Art of Worship* could easily be a faith-based inspirational how-to book rather than the humorous teenage deflowering story it really is. In fact, if you do an Amazon search on "the art of worship", you'll find alongside mine quite a few religious books. I didn't choose my titles to purposely fly under the radar. But titles that sound more literary are likely to reduce the risk of flags.

- TRUTH IN ADVERTISING. Unless there's blatant irony in your intention, don't call your book about a consensual sex-only arrangement *Sweethearts in Love*. The idea isn't to mislead readers, but to exercise judgment and understand the impacts of those choices in terms of how they position your books.

WHEN TITLE DOESN'T MATTER

Some books will be flagged regardless of their titles. This is where category classifications come in. If you categorize your book as erotic romance, you've let the cat out of the bag. Do this on Amazon, and they will automatically lock you out of advertising, regardless of what keywords your title and blurb may or may not contain. But if your intention is to get a pass and a milder category is a true-enough option, tone your searchable text down. Playing up the heat level of your novel—and getting banned for it—will feel like a crippling consequence if you're up against authors who are not doing the same.

BLURBING HOT BOOKS

It's hard enough to write the blurb for any book, and books with erotic content have unique challenges. Here, I'll define a book blurb as any descriptive text that appears in core spaces meant to describe the plot of the book. This includes book descriptions that appear on back covers, those that appear between cover images and order buttons on retail sites, and descriptions that appear to the right of covers and below titles on Goodreads.

On a site like Goodreads, which is not a direct source of retail sales, guidelines may be less stringent, or at least appear to be mostly unenforced. But for digital retailers, authors don't have free rein over the kind of descriptive language that is used. At the time of the writing of this book, the Kindle Direct Publishing Content Guidelines on Amazon specified that "book titles, cover art and product descriptions" must not contain "pornography or offensive depictions of graphic sexual acts." It goes on to vaguely prohibit offensive content, saying (unhelpfully) that "What we deem offensive is probably about what you would expect."

Enticing your target, warning those who will find your content undesirable, and satisfying retailers are distinct goals that often stand at odds. Readers will look for clues that they'll love it, but they don't necessarily want spoilers or disclaimers that will give too much away. By contrast, other readers need warnings, and by "other readers" I mean those who aren't open to certain themes. Retailers and advertisers want blurbs to be utterly accurate (and there are reasons why you should want this, too). Yet, admitting in black and white terms that your book contains explicit content will often buck against the policies of platforms you rely on. How and where you plan to advertise should dictate your approach in writing the blurb for your book.

LANGUAGE: KEYWORDS VS. TRIGGER WORDS

Language is a biggie. If your plan is to advertise on major platforms, weed out the crudest terms that could be used to describe your taboo. Think of every technical term and euphemism you know to describe your theme—then think of ways to present your book without using any of them.

A blurb I love (one so good it made me buy the book) is the description for Sybil Bartel's novel, *Thrust*. It is a masterful example of saying it without *saying it*, and is utterly devoid of trigger words. Her hero, Alex, is a gigolo. Instead of using the word gigolo or escort, or even writing the blurb in the third person, she uses first person and speaks from Alex's point of view. She gives us phrases like "Ten inches of real estate never felt so good," and "My client list is long and my motto is short— one single thrust and you're mine." These two sentences alone tell us a *ton* about the genre, let us hear the character's voice and do their job of making the prospective reader want to buy the book *right now*. Because a robot will usually be the first gate- keeper intended to sniff out your book for red flags, it's smart to use a blurb that's utterly devoid of key phrases that might trip the wire.

The point is, be creative. Even when it feels as if there is no way to avoid trigger words, think hard to uncover options. In a book about a sex arrangement, you don't have to use the words "sex arrangement" or even "friends with benefits". Substituting keywords like those with ones like "no-strings-attached" or "no- commitment" relationship are easy switches. To be even subtler, craft a descriptive sentence that dances around it more. For example: "He doesn't mind waking up with her in his arms or enduring the prying eyes of her neighbor on his way out. What- ever happens in the dark of night, by the light of morning, they go back to being friends." If writing blurbs isn't your forte, hire someone to do it for you. If you don't care about trigger words, signal away.

My novel that could not be advertised on mainstream chan- nels took an opposite approach. My blurb reads: "The rules are simple: toe-curling sex, unattached companionship, and a clean break when it all ends. Either one can say the single word that will end it: *snapdragon*." With the decision made to go the purist route, I opened the door to be able to write a more explicit blurb.

The other opportunity with language choice relates to peppering keywords into your description. Even if you don't have trope signals in your title, working them into the description will still help your book in organic search. Here, think in terms of key phrases you can weave in. If they don't flow naturally, feel free to use them after the primary blurb. For example, on a new line after the teaser-style blurb, you can write a stand-alone sentence, such as "a friends with benefits millionaire romance".

CHAPTER THREE

REQUIRED AND OPTIONAL DISCLOSURES

D o you see a pattern forming? The core issue that decides whether you win or lose points, and with who, is always signaling. No gatekeeper is going to curl up and read your book to figure out what it contains — they're going to trust the clues. Similarly, not all readers will be paying close attention in the moments when they're considering a purchase. This chapter covers disclosures in the order that authors are asked, or given the opportunity, to provide them.

WHEN YOU CREATE YOUR BOOK

Most required disclosures are covered at the time when you set up your book. When uploading your manuscript to Smashwords, Amazon and most retailers, you will be asked whether your book contains mature content. This is certainly true for ebook retailers. Even for print-only books, category signals are required when setting up an ISBN. Asking authors to self-identify their content as mature is the first gate in the system.

I'm gonna keep it real. A lot of authors simply lie. When I complained to friends about being in advertising jail, every single one of them told me that checking the mature content box on KDP had been a mistake. The ethics of this are pretty clear. When you check the box at the end of the legalese you agree to when you set up your account, you're agreeing to be honest and exposing yourself to ramifications if you misrepresent your book.

This dynamic leaves authors with bad incentives. Most happily-ever-after romance nowadays gives readers a detailed look at what happens in the bedroom. Should authors do what everyone else is doing and have a shot at competing, or be honest and shoot themselves in the foot? This is where your personal moral compass comes in. I can't tell you what to do. Just know that a critical mass of authors has stayed out of jail by the simple act of not telling the truth.

CHOOSING BOOK CATEGORIES

Genre categorizations are perhaps the most abused signal in the retailer universe. If you write in this genre and don't live in a cave, even you know that tens of thousands of books that are without-a-question erotica are categorized as contemporary romance. The definition of erotica that I skew towards is one in which the plot could not exist in the absence of sexual events or themes portrayed in the book. Light-on-plot and heavy-on-sex is a phase the romance genre has been going through for at least ten years.

Most authors who meddle with otherwise intuitive categorizations are doing it to game the system. Put a book in Fiction >> Romance>> Contemporary Romance and on your best day, you'll never make it into the top 100. Put it in an obscure category like Historical >> Shifters >> Hidden Pregnancy and you'll soon be a category bestseller! (Note: thank God, there is no real sub-category called Historical >> Shifters >> Hidden Pregnancy. I'm a little sarcastic, so that's an example I just used for illustrative purposes. Hopefully, you'll now what I mean).

As an author of steamy content, the decision you have to

make is which category is most accurate. I made the mistake of believing that I had to categorize *Snapdragon* as Erotica. It's a friends-with-benefits sex arrangement and because it fit my own definition of what erotica is, I felt obliged to disclose it. It's steamy, to be sure, but on that ever-important spectrum, the heat level is not extreme. The truth is, it was better-aligned to the expectations of readers in Contemporary Romance.

My novella, *The Art of Worship*, is similar. It's a super-awkward comedy about a teenager who wants to lose his v-card with his girlfriend but realizes that he needs sex advice from his dad. The plot is undoubtedly reliant upon sex, but it's written more to make people laugh and feel nostalgic about being in high school than it is to tantalize. This is where you have to put on your thinking cap and make your own decision about what your category should be. I did not, by the way, categorize that one as erotica. Someone in the market for a real erotica novella would be utterly disappointed.

OPTIONAL DISCLOSURES: WARNINGS IN BLURBS

Five years ago, it was uncommon to see warnings and disclaimers tacked onto book descriptions. Nowadays, steamy romance novel descriptions seem overrun with end notes that seem to say "buyer, beware". Angry readers who discover elements they simply didn't expect take liberties in expressing their dissatisfaction. And, by "dissatisfaction", what I mean is bad reviews.

For an author, the incentive to place warnings up front is to avoid selling books to the wrong reader. The problem is, warnings can give plot reveals away. I've seen books with so many plot reveals covered in the warning that it killed my motivation to read it. With all told up front, I was doubtful that any surprises would await.

Yet, there are legitimate reasons to consider adding warnings. What I'll kindly call ditzy reviewers are people who give bad reviews because they ignored signals about what they would find. Putting a big, bold, all caps note at the end of your book description on a retail site is extra insurance that the wrong person won't buy and that if they do, then give you a bad review, you can appeal the review on the grounds that they'd been warned (more on this later).

Trigger warnings are trickier and avoiding them can be a tough decision. I mention these specifically, as some of the mature themes that fall under the spectrum of erotic writing can involve things like non-con (which, in real life, I always call what I believe it to be—rape—but which I realize is a recognized sub-area of erotica) and darker sexual themes.

It's kind to be sensitive to readers who simply can't handle certain content. I'll admit that I don't like reading stories in which a kid dies or in which somebody is mean to pets. I would never give a story a bad review because it had the audacity to punch me in the gut with a trigger. But I'm not most readers, and there are plenty who will slam you for that.

My personal approach is to be sensitive to victims, but not to let other petty things get in the way. If my book has a rape, or the death of a child, or any tragedy that real people suffer, I'd sooner sell fewer books than make a prospective reader relive a real life painful event. What I won't do is bend over backwards to restate things that have already been made obvious. I won't specify that my book ends in a cliffhanger if it's clear from the title that it's part of a series. I won't rewrite that it contains adult content, because reading the description should make it clear.

CHAPTER FOUR

CREATING ADS AND VIDEO TRAILERS

We've covered decisions you'll face about the core characteristics of your book—the things that determine how it will look and where it will be featured. With product assets out of the way, let's talk about supporting assets and ads. This is the set of materials you develop to help drive awareness of your brand or to drive users to take action on a book you want them to buy. In this section I'll be covering how to create a handful of assets with a still graphical format, from banners to postings to flat ads.

The basic principles that apply to your product elements also apply to assets like these. Art and language that's too racy will get disapproved from ads. In other places where you decide to place non-ad content (e.g., postings on Instagram, Twitter, Facebook, Tumblr and even content within your newsletter), you still run the risk of someone reporting you and having your post or your profile banned.

DISPLAY AD HACK #1: GO RACIER NEARLY EVERYWHERE ELSE

As I mention above, using steamy text and images can always piss someone off and get you reported and banned. With that said, what's generally accepted on the user pages and feeds (not ads) on the aforementioned social sites is a lot looser than anything you'll be held to by retailers and advertisers. Particularly on a platform where you don't plan to advertise, posting your racier content can be easier, and can help you do whatever signaling you want as a part of connecting with your readers.

Let's say Amazon wouldn't let you use male frontal nudity on your book cover (and I don't mean a nice chest and ripped abs). No problem! Set up a Tumblr. They really don't give a shit. Also, because you won't advertise your Tumblr, you run no risk of Tumblr having an opinion on the maturity level of your account and rejecting any ads you might try to run based on its visibility into your content.

DISPLAY AD HACK #2: FORGET YOUR COVER FOR ADS

If your cover is too racy to be approved as part of an ad, don't be hasty to give up completely on major platform advertising. There's no law that says an ad for a book has to show the cover at all. You've got a shot at being approved for advertising by using tamer art as an alternative. For example, ads featuring my book covers routinely get rejected, but I get by using other images that relate to the book. For *Snapdragon*, I have an ad that has a suited male model who fits the description of my hero. It's a different model and image that's used than the naked-from-the-waist-up model that dons the cover of my book. Similarly, the stock photo that was used on my cover of *The Art of Worship* has been successful as an ad image when I showed a different part of the image and did some editing.

The point here is, be creative. If you don't choose a cover that makes advertising easy, go back to the drawing board on other art. Stock photos don't cost very much. If you try an image that's disapproved, just find another. Tweak and optimize until you find one that can work. Your cover isn't the only image in town. Giving up too soon on creative solutions could mean the difference between advertising, or not advertising, your book on the big platforms.

Full disclosure: whether this will work is dependent on what's on the landing page for the ad. Part of what ad platforms are doing when they're forcing ads to pass approval is making sure the ad and the destination aren't misaligned. For example, they don't want someone to put an ad up for a Christian singles dating site and then have that ad link to a gay sex porn site. The approval process will be screening for evidence that the destination isn't unsuitable. There's a chance that a gatekeeper will take one look at your racy cover on the retailer website your ad links to and conclude that the ad can't be approved.

DISPLAY AD HACK #3: DON'T BE AFRAID OF SUBTLETY

I know humans can be dumb sometimes, but don't underestimate the power of suggestion. You can have a very sexy and provocative brand without art that shows a lot of skin and shoves it in everyone's face. Remember, everyone means *everyone*. If the sex is super-obvious to your followers, it will also be super-obvious to gatekeepers. Dylan Cross has a book called *Amanda's Birthday* that has a white background with a red silk ribbon curled and draped on the front. Make your assets like the Simpsons—funny and innocent enough for kids but subtle enough that only the grown-ups get the jokes.

CREATING VIDEO TRAILERS

Video trailers can be a great way to build your follower base and sell your books. One thing I like about video is that it becomes what is called an evergreen asset. Other ad types you run are only available when a campaign is live. But a video trailer can have a permanent place on your web site or a YouTube channel. You can even embed them in newsletters, post them to your social media pages, or in other places that may encourage readers to buy. In this sense, video ads create opportunities for the asset to perform in numerous places.

But, remember—rules against explicit or mature content are the same for video as they are for book covers and ads. For authors of erotic romance, the best idea is to work up different versions. First and foremost, make sure your core video asset is not so steamy that it won't pass even the most lenient video posting rules. Even if you're just slapping it up on YouTube, your Facebook page, or your website, it's possible for viewers to report it, and for the site you're serving it off of to have it banned.

Advertising, of course, is a different story. Video ads tend to work best when they are thirty seconds or less, and when they pack as much punch as possible in the beginning. If a video isn't exciting enough right from the start, viewers are likely to stop watching it. The other best practice is to include a call to action. At the end of the video, you want to tell the user what to do. For advertising, you may want to make several versions: a pre-sale version that encourages viewers to pre-order, a variation that encourages viewers to order once the book is available for general sale, or if you want to use the video to grow your mailing list, you may want to put an offer at the end, maybe a giveaway that requires an e-mail signup.

Also, platform matters. Depending on where you are placing the video, there may be an opportunity to write accompanying content. This is true on Facebook and Twitter. On YouTube, depending on the video format, you may be able to add something called a companion banner next to the ad. In general, video ads are cost-efficient. Most platforms charge advertisers only when a certain number of seconds of the video is viewed. If you put enough great content in the first few seconds, you will build awareness and maybe sales even among viewers who didn't stick around to watch the whole thing.

With that said, producing video or buying stock video can be an expensive proposition. I made a pretty sweet trailer for Snapdragon using iMovie, but the stock footage cost me close to $500 for the three different clips I use and I burnt a whole day of my time. My plan was to use it as an ad unit, and I learned what I've just told you the hard way (my video was rejected by both Facebook and YouTube for advertising). You don't want to invest a ton of money with the idea to promote it only to discover that the finished product can't get approved as an ad.

The time and money that I spent was on a single version of a 30-second video. Had I created variations, it would have cost me more money for cleaner video clips and at least another day of my own time. Supposing you don't have the skills to create your own trailer, a good video will cost you similarly, or maybe even more.

HIGH-QUALITY VS. HIGH-CONCEPT

Not all high-quality video trailers have to be high-concept. Something simple will do just fine if the quality is good. When planning your video, don't feel as if the storyboard has to be a literal summary of your book. The key is to develop a fetching storyboard, and a combination of great music, tantalizing copy, and even just one killer video clip can go a long way. The key here is to think about selling points—the plot summary is only one possibility. Depending on what accolades you have to brag about, focusing on those could be just fine. Use positive quotes from critical reviews or talk about bestseller status or awards you've won. The idea is to convince the reader that they're in for a phenomenal book. Consider using every tool in your toolkit to tell a visual story that will help you achieve that goal.

THE TITLE-AGNOSTIC TRAILER

Video trailers also don't have to be specific to a single book, though some authors live by that approach. If you have numerous titles available, or if you write a certain kind of book, you can make an author trailer. Particularly if your book covers don't pass advertising guidelines for mature content, consider making a more general trailer about why a reader may want to read your books. In a video like that, you can use art and sequencing that does not require the use of your covers.

PART TWO

GOING OFF-SCRIPT

CHAPTER FIVE

E-MAIL LISTS AND NEWSLETTERS

As we shift into the set of tactics that any author can use, regardless of creative strategy, e-mail lists are the perfect place to start. Since users opt in, your newsletters provide you with the most leeway to include anything you want.

That doesn't mean there aren't gatekeepers—only different ones. Unless you're sending mass e-mails directly from your inbox, you'll still have a mail service like MailChimp or MailerLite to deal with. Those services are sensitive to making sure you're not a spammer. In that sense you don't want to send mail to people who have not, in fact, opted in, nor do you want to send anything that a persnickety list member is likely to view as offensive or mark as spam.

That part requires management. If you don't want anyone to get her panties in a twist about something you send out, make sure that anywhere readers have a chance to opt in, you're telling them what to expect. If you're going to send an e-mail daily, make sure readers know that. If you don't, you're more likely to piss off someone who feels spammed. If you plan to deliver super-steamy reads and heavy up on the sexy stuff, make sure folks know that ahead of time and have a chance to pass.

SEXY STUFF AND SPAM FILTERS

Even if your list members want the sexy stuff, you still have to be a little careful with the language your messages contain. Sexy keywords may cause mail servers to mark your messages as spam. We have the pornography industry to thank for that. Your own spam filter likely serves as evidence of this. You're not hawking penis enlargement or live nude girls, but sexy words used in your titles and message bodies might raise a flag. Having your mail end up in spam filters could be a larger problem than you think. Maybe you have a mailing list of 10,000 subscribers, but if 5,000 messages per send end up in spam boxes it will erode your results. Followers can't buy books they can't see, making e-mail messages another place to be conscious of wording.

EARNING NEW SUBSCRIBERS THROUGH FREEBIES

Depending on what you're willing to do to earn them, finding subscribers can be easy. The most tried-and-true way to build your list is by using freebies. The basic logic is that readers may be more willing to try out an author they've never read if they're able to get the book for free. No reader feels good about having paid money for a book they didn't like. An initial freebie lets readers take a chance on a new author without financial risk. For authors, there is risk. Some takers rarely pay for books—they just hop from freebie to freebie. If you're lucky, they unsubscribe. If you're not, they remain on your list as dead weight who will never buy from you after the initial book.

There are two ways to deal with readers like this. The first is to make your free book the first in a series—preferably a series with a cliffhanger. I know that some other wisdom recommends starting readers on a novella, but if it's short, it's not really showing how well you can make a novel come together and if it's a standalone, it presents too much of an opportunity for a dead end. You may have missed out on royalties from book one, but with a book two in the mix you'll make something on the investment. And don't use just any old book—give away the first installment of your best series. This could mean the difference between lukewarm appreciation for a freebie and earning a long-term reader.

The second way to deal with readers who download an initial freebie but don't buy is to be diligent about list-cleaning. This refers to weeding out followers who simply aren't responding to your messages anymore. This calls back to the reason to use a mail service like MailChimp or MailerLite to administer your sends. These services give you stats on who's opening, who's clicking, and if your tracking is set up well, you can even see who's buying. Diligent list-cleaning will reduce the size of your list but it will also make sure that you're building a higher-quality community of readers. To the extent that the mail services charge based on how many messages you're sending out each month, and to how many users, list-cleaning reduces costs. There are other ways to leverage the e-mail addresses of users you might have cleaned out. I save every e-mail address I've ever collected—cleaned or not—for use with Facebook custom audiences.

As for where to find subscribers, put your book up on freebie sites. Services like Instafreebie and Bookfunnel charge a monthly fee to host giveaway pages and collect e-mails on your behalf. The better sites let you require readers to verify their e-mail addresses before accessing the freebie. Matchmaking for group promotions are a perk on some of these sites. Dozens of author-run Facebook groups also facilitate group giveaways. Do a search for "Instafreebie erotica" or "Bookfunnel erotica" on Facebook and you'll find many. Sometimes the organizers of promos such as these have requirements (e.g., all books have to be about shifters, all authors need mailing lists of at least 4,000, etc.). The common expectation is that each participating author will dedicate a newsletter to sending out links to the group's collection of books.

Some group promos charge money for participation. Bex Dane, for example, runs a promo called BuzzBooks. Participants agree to the newsletter swapping described above, but premium services such as hers offer additional perks. For one, she screens all of the books that make it in for quality and ratings. She hosts a landing page that saves authors time they would have spent custom-linking their newsletters and promotes the landing page through her own channels for a month.

The important thing here is to make sure that you choose freebie swaps that align to your erotic genre. If you write paranormal, you don't want to participate in a giveaway that's focused on new adult. Another factor impacting results is the list size of the other authors participating, and how many books there will be. A mega-swap with more than 20 or 30 books could cause yours to get lost in the shuffle.

OTHER WAYS TO EARN NEW SUBSCRIBERS

This is pretty basic wisdom, but if you aren't shilling your mailing list at the end of each book, putting a link on your social media pages and actively posting a link to the list every once in awhile, and placing a signup box on your web site, why the hell not? People can't join a list they don't know about, so make sure people know that it's there. When you go to book signings, conferences, and even networking events with other authors, pass out a card or a bookmark with a QR code that drives people to a freebie for joining your list.

Another way to get your mailing list in front of people is to get on the circuit with other authors. Participate in takeovers and release parties and seek out opportunities to be blurbed or write guest postings on other authors' blogs. Every author who is hustling his marketing program is starving for content and participation.

WHAT IF YOU DON'T WANT TO USE FREEBIES?

Unrestricted newsletter swaps are a lever you might want to pull if you don't want to be locked into freebies. If authors only ever talked about their own books in newsletters, their content would bore their readers to tears. Consequently, authors with high volume newsletters are always looking for other authors to work with on trade. Authors want to feature other authors who write in their genre, who have lists at least as large as theirs, and who can commit to featuring their books on a date that works within the marketing framework of a specific book. These authors generally will not require you to set your book's price point to free as a condition of promoting it.

With that said, there's a lot of junk out there. A newsletter with 10,000 readers isn't worth much if the author features ten books with each send, and sends daily. With nine other books to compete with in the same newsletter, among a list of subscribers who are being shown seventy books a week, your book is less likely to receive the desired love. Also, even if you can feature your book at full price, if the newsletter itself is full of freebies, it could hurt your book's chances of earning a try.

Finally, there's quality to consider. I know it's tempting to swap with an author who's bigger than you and who might have a list that's double your list's size. But if you're writing good quality fiction in a certain sub-genre, and they're putting out a crappy book every few weeks, pass. Their readers probably aren't your readers. More importantly, including them in your newsletter puts you in the awkward position of telling your own followers, who you've fought to build trust and rapport with, to read something you know doesn't meet their standard. After all, they're not in love with just-any-novels—they're in love with novels like yours.

On the other hand, if you get an opportunity to swap with an author who doesn't send out as frequently, who only promotes one or two other books with each newsletter, and who seems to align with your work in terms of quality, jump on it. Build meaningful relationships with these types of authors, as these are the ones who you really want to do all sorts of cross-promotion with. Invite well-aligned authors to participate in your own launch-party takeovers. Read their books and feel good about recommending them to your readers in good faith.

CREATING YOUR OWN NEWSLETTER OPPORTUNITIES

You don't have to wait for a group promo bandwagon to jump on or for another author to approach you. Once you figure out which authors align to your brand, approach them first, and make a good case for why they should form an alliance with you. There are a few ways to figure out what authors are similar to you. Checking out the "customers also bought" section at the bottom of an Amazon page is one place to start. Also, you can do an author search for yourself on web sites like eReaderIQ, which gives a word cloud as a visual list of authors who have some affinity to you. Not all authors you see on the list may be conducive to approaching. My biggest hit is Sherrilyn Kenyon, and I also got hits from authors who don't write in my genre. You could also do it the old-fashioned way and simply ask people who know your work—from editors who have worked on your manuscripts, to friends, to readers—which authors they view as similar to you.

When taking this approach, screen first. It's a win if you find authors whose books you really love. Becoming mutual fans and mutual promoters is the ideal, but if that doesn't happen, it's okay. When reaching out, write a brief, but friendly, pitch letter stating what you bring to the table, as well as any other information (awards, ratings, accolades) that demonstrate the quality of your work and ask whether the author would be open to a trade.

And don't be afraid to approach an author who's doing better than you. In some cases, that author won't be in control of her own marketing, but you never know who you might get. Very few of us are overnight successes. Some of the most generous help I've received in the publishing world has been from authors who were much bigger than me.

FINAL NOTE: WATCH OUT FOR SCAMMERS

It sucks that I have to write a section like this, but it's sound advice to be careful. I've been approached by big authors (or their PAs) who I don't know personally to do newsletter swaps, only to do mine first and never hear from them again. These aren't contractually-protected covenants—they're casual arrangements between humans, and some of the humans involved are unethical people. In two cases, I googled these authors later with the word "scam" and found that I hadn't been the first. As you navigate choppy marketing waters, it's always smart to have a friend or two who keep their ears to the ground and know who to look out for. If you're feeling unsure, ask friends and go to Google to check strangers out.

CHAPTER SIX

GETTING THE MOST OUT OF YOUR WEB SITE

W eb sites are another asset in your marketing ecosystem over which you'll maintain a high degree of control. This is another place to say whatever you want, show whatever art you want, produce whatever video you want (you get the picture) in relation to your books and your brand. Maybe the super-sexy stock photo you passed on for your cover would be perfect for a web site graphic like a section background or the header for your blog. Your web site presents endless opportunities for you to solidify your brand and show people who you are. If you own your own domain and are paying for your own hosting, you'll find very few restrictions around the kind of content you can post. If you've been writhing and squirming, just waiting to get freaky, your web site will give you your chance.

For readers, sexier might be better. But your web site isn't just for readers. Just about anyone in the industry may have an interest in checking you out. This chapter is about understanding your full range of website audiences and being strategic about how you want to craft your brand.

A LITANY OF AUDIENCES

Most authors think of their websites in terms of direct marketing or relationship marketing. That is, they view them as a place to help readers feel connected to them and find their books. Though this is true, some of the biggest breaks in an author's career come not from individual readers, but from other players in the industry who may be sizing them up.

I'll never forget the very first pitch meeting I did. After another author didn't show for her 10-minute pitch appointment at a big conference, I'd gotten in with an editor I wasn't scheduled to see. Even as I sat in front of her, I wasn't sure which book I would pitch. Because I wasn't expecting the meeting, I also wasn't as well-studied as I could've been on the publisher. Stalling for a few seconds, I offered her my card. Instead of diving right into asking me for my pitch, she paused, not-so-subtly smiling as her eyes lit up. She fingered the thick white card with my elegant logo and sassy pink border. She was delighted a second time when she turned the card over and found a summary of my genres, five resplendent stars to showcase my ratings, and a QR code offering a download of one of my books. "I like this," she said with emphasis, before we moved onto the pitch (at the close of the meeting, she asked for my manuscript, by the way). Through my marketer glasses, I saw immediately how my small, awesome business card had won me points.

Bluntly, good writing doesn't sell books—only good marketing does. Gone are the days of walking into B. Dalton Bookseller and lingering for a half an hour to scrutinize covers, read blurbs and inevitably walk out of the store with whatever book a big publisher thought was good enough for retail shelves. Today's readers have options, but they're also overwhelmed. They look hard at peer validation. If your web site makes it clear that you have readers, and good ratings, it will make you more attractive to just about everybody. Authors with influence are the most important authors to know.

What this means for your website is that a number of stakeholders interested in your writing career may visit with the express purpose of understanding how well you're managing your brand. As you think about crafting your website, think about a spectrum of audiences you may be trying to impress, and what they need to see in order to leave your site more excited about you than they were when they arrived.

- **AGENTS AND EDITORS.** To riff off of points mentioned above, agents and editors may want to know more about you. If you're actively pitching, be sure your website is set up to speak to them. Maybe they loved your manuscript—now they need to get a sense for your brand. Is the manuscript you submitted aligned with other things you write? What other books have you written and how are the ratings? Are you self-published or were your previous books signed to other publishers? How active are you around posting and reaching your audience? These are logical questions. An agent who is considering trying to sell your manuscript won't just be selling your book to publishers—she'll be selling your entire brand. Editors considering adding you to their bench will want to check you out to make sure, among other things, that your image is on-brand for their house. Before deciding whether to invest in you, they'll want to find out whether you're more trouble to gussy up than their time is worth.

- **OTHER AUTHORS.** If you think other authors don't check you out, you, sir or madam, are mistaken. The biggest stalkers—I mean, snoops—erm...the most dedicated researchers I've ever met are authors. Some are just curious, but there are a ton of totally legit reasons for why another author may head to your website. Maybe they clicked on a blog posting you wrote that got shared around or they want to partner up on an anthology and they want to check out your brand. Maybe they read a good pro-tip you offered up in a Facebook group and want to see what you're all about. If you've got content for authors—maybe a newsletter swap, a book review blog, a side editing business or really, anything, craft your navigation in a way that shows authors were to go.

- **READERS.** Readers who have heard your name but who haven't read you just yet want to get a barometer for what you write. They'll be reacting to images and text to figure out your genres and tropes and they'll want to understand heat level. More than agents, editors and authors, readers will have a shorter attention span when it comes to reading the copy on your site. They may want to know less about you personally than they do about your books. They might not read the "about the author" page that tells them you write erotic romance and romantic suspense, but if a strong header banner nails it, they'll get the picture. Those who have read you might want to get a broader sense for your brand. That first book they read was great—now what else can they read? Unless you write the exact same kind of book over and over, your website has to show readers key differences between each of your books.

CHAPTER SEVEN

PAID ADVERTISING WITH NICHE PLAYERS

By contrast to major advertising platforms, niche players deal on a smaller scale. They may have extraordinary influence over getting readers to buy, but they're not mass market players. Because they cater only to authors and readers, they understand the publishing space and are many times less restrictive to authors in terms of policies. This section introduces 3 types of niche advertising channels that work well for erotic authors.

BOOK PROMOTION SITES

For the purposes of this book, I'll define book promotion sites as websites that charge a fee for listings. They distinguish themselves by doing these four important things: 1) They cultivate a base of differentiated subscribers whose reading habits they understand, 2) They aggregate recommendations for discrete groups of readers, 3) They allow authors who meet certain criteria to pay for a guaranteed placement, and 4) They employ a "push" strategy to spread the word. Fortunately for us, a *lot* of book promotion sites accept erotic romance. Here are some things to think about as you consider whether to promote on these sites:

THE PROS AND CONS OF BOOK PROMOTION SITES

The great thing about book promotion sites is that readers opt in based on their preferences. Users typically join these sites because they want book suggestions within the genres they like to read. Most readers are led to believe that by subscribing to the service, they'll be receiving a daily digest of what books are new and hot. If they haven't taken the time to poke around and figure out how these sites work, they have no idea that most books (if not every book) being recommended is a paid advertisement.

Yet, these readers buy books. They take these recommendations. And they tend to be voracious readers (after all, only a voracious reader would subscribe to a service that sent them a list of recommendations every single day). Fortunately for us, romance readers have a habit of buying books that look interesting to them, whether they plan to read immediately or not. Most romance readers I know complain that their "to be read" list is a mile long.

For steamy and erotic romance authors, this is a big win. Many of these sites maintain separate lists for people who like contemporary romance vs. people who like erotic romance. Red Feather Romance, for example, focuses exactly where its name would cause you to expect: it targets readers who like the steamy stuff. Red *Roses* Romance, on the other hand, makes a distinction between romance and erotica and has no genre focus outside of those two. Sites like BargainBooksy are even broader, featuring romance as one of a dozen genres such as Non-Fiction, Thriller, and Religion.

What I like is that everyone you will reach is open to (and possibly prefers) really steamy reads. Particularly if you skew toward promotion sites that cater specifically to erotica readers, yur covers will not be banned, your descriptions won't be flagged, and (I'm just being really honest) even books with highly controversial themes might make it through. Sites like this are in business to make money and they only hit top ROI when every ad slot is sold out every day. Unless your book has some flagrant taboo (like the word "fuck" in the name or naked genitals on the cover), you're unlikely to be rejected on the basis of assets alone.

What I don't like about these sites is that not all of them offer premium placement. Most of them send out between five and ten recommendations in each category per day. You may purchase an ad only to find, on the day of the promo, that your book is dead last. If luck is on your side you may just as easily discover that your book is at the top of the list. The point is, with some of these services, you have no control over the position of your placement and you may end up disappointed in results. In most of the advertising industry, ad position is considered very important, yet some of these sites charge flat pricing for placements and turn a blind eye to whether position factors in.

I've observed other things I can't confirm. For example, I've seen best-selling authors closer to the top. Maybe their publishers (or the authors themselves) are making back room deals for better placement. Maybe the promoters are cherry-picking authors with name recognition so that their readers feel confident that they're not getting junk. I've also seen books with better covers, or books in sub-genres that are hot get better placement than books that appear less marketable. The way to get around all of this is to choose promotion sites that have a "book of the day" option, or some other placement that will get you closer to the top.

REVIEW THRESHOLDS

Some book promotion sites have a review threshold. The one I see most often is 3.5 but some require 4.5 stars or more. If your book has an Amazon rating lower than that, promotion sites may flatly reject your book. I've also seen sites that require a certain number of reviews, or a certain number of reviews for premium placements. This is another example of promoters trying to junk-proof the inboxes of their subscribers. They are hedging to protect the value of their recommendations, and guarding against shilling books their subscribers aren't going to like.

DEAL-SWEETENERS

Some packages include deal-sweeteners (often for an additional fee), such as an author interview, a blog posting, or extra social media broadcasts about your book. For example, a basic placement may be $30, but for an additional $15 you may get extra coverage on that day or throughout the week. One way to assess the value of these deal-sweeteners is to check out engagement. If a site is trying to upsell you extra social media coverage for a fee, take a look at their social media. What I've noticed is that some of these pages have nearly no engagement. It may be worth it if every posting is getting twenty likes or shares. It's not at all worth it if you listen to their page and hear crickets.

The two premium placements I love are blog articles and "book of the day" type placements. If the blog articles are permanently archived, they become an asset that you can add to your own web site's media page. Your readers won't know that you paid for a placement in such-and-such blog that covered you. Showing that you're important enough for a book site to interview you or write an article about your book underscores your value as an author.

Finally, top positioning and "book of the day" type placements may be worth the extra cash. Again, if your book is the last one on the list, there's no guarantee that readers who open the e-mail will even scroll down that far. They act as insurance that the people who take the time to check out the e-mail will at least see your book. Again, all advertising industry wisdom points to the fact that a better position translates to better sales.

SALES PLATFORMS

Another thing to consider is what platforms the promo site links to. Some of them only link to Amazon, which means that on the day of your promo, you will only sell books on Kindle. This is fine if you're dedicated to KU, but if you want to increase your reader base on iBooks, Barnes & Noble, Kobo, Scribd, Google Play, and others, you may want to consider this before you choose.

DEAL OR NO DEAL?

Finally, some promo sites are focused on deals—in other words, they only carry books that are discounted and they often have very specific guidelines around what your sale price must be, depending on the original price. The biggest danger, when discounting your book, is to be mindful of audience profile. Some people are cheapskates who are just looking to get free and $0.99 books. Some authors don't have a problem with giving a book away for free if it means they get to earn a reader. A worthy counterpoint predicts that any reader who cares about great deals or a free lunch is not the kind of reader who will ever pay money for your book.

The bigger book promo sites tend to have different ad prices for books that are regular price vs. discounted vs. free. Do the math on these. If you make $2 more per sale in royalties by NOT discounting your book, you have to sell fewer books to break even on the promotion. Additionally, by selling your book at full price, you may be attracting readers who are willing to pay real money for books they like. Readers who like to pay full price? It doesn't get better than that.

I don't like to discount too deeply, but I would be remiss if I didn't mention BookBub. Be willing to discount your book significantly if you apply to be featured on this site. If you're lucky enough to earn a placement, BookBub's dedicated base of readers is known to buy promoted books in the hundreds. I've never met an author who didn't recoup the fees he paid for the promotion on the same day.

ADVANCED STRATEGY: MAKE YOUR BOOK TREND

Authors aren't just using book promo sites to sell books on random days of the year—they're stacking placements on specific days to manipulate their rankings. I don't mean to cast the word "manipulate" in a bad light—timing advertising campaigns with specific goals in mind—usually a strong launch —is something that advertisers in every industry hold in mind. If you subscribe to enough book promo services, you'll see which authors are advertising on numerous sites. Authors who invest heavily in this tactic could easily spend $1,500 per week. The ones who do are meticulous at timing, and tend to trend very well.

Trending packs a triple-whammy in terms of marketing appeal. Maintain top rankings for long enough, and your book will reach bestseller status. Even if you don't care about those bragging rights, high rankings will win you a halo effect among readers who browse lists of top sellers and make buying decisions based on what's hot. Even if you only reached the top of the list because of well-timed promotions, selling halo effect books might give you a chance to linger there for awhile.

PRICING AND RESULTS

Services like these can be found in the dozens. Pricing (and certainly results) will vary. I've promoted all three of my fiction books. Even within that group, certain books performed better than others. All of my books had star ratings above 4.5, but the top performer was the only one with more than seventy-five reviews, which made it eligible to be featured on some very high-performing promotion sites that had higher review minimums. It also had the strongest cover and the pithiest blurb. The other two books got significantly different results.

I've paid as little as $9 on a single promotion that sold fourteen books and as much as $150 on a single promotion that sold fifteen. Among sites that have consistently performed for me, I've paid an average of $91 per promotion to sell 53 books. After netting out immediate royalties earned on initial sales, the average direct loss drops to $49. On promotions with this cost profile, I need to earn an additional $0.93 per reader on royalties from subsequent books to recoup my investment. But not every reader who buys the first book will move on to the second, or the third. Let's assume that 25% of those who bought my starter book go on to buy the other two books in my library. In order to break even in that case, I would need to earn a total of $3.70 in royalties per reader who became a fan.

In Part 3, I'll talk about figuring out campaign Return on Investment (ROI) by calculating the Total Lifetime Value(TLV) of a reader. Campaigns like this rarely look ROI-positive at the beginning, but if you can step people through your library using effective upselling, they are rarely a loss. As with all marketing tactics, you will have to figure out which promo site audiences are well-aligned to your writing, and schedule placements in a way that won't overexpose you or burn readers out.

CHOOSING BOOK PROMOTION SITES

In addition to BargainBooksy, Red Feather Romance and Red Roses Romance, Booksends, Robin Reads, and Crave Romance all offer erotic or steamy romance promotions. Services that do not have an erotic category include Many-Books, eBookSoda, and eReader News Today. I've gottenn good (and bad) results from all sorts of promo sites, no matter the audience focus. Head to www.marketingsteamyromance.com for an up-to-date index of book promotion services. Beyond the dozen or more that I've tried personally, the list of sites I'm aware of is simply too log to elegantly name.

———

PAID BLOG PLACEMENTS

Bloggers are a different story. For one, bloggers rarely have differentiated reader bases who they are sending materials to in a targeted way. Whereas a book promotion site might roadblock you the second you arrive onto the home page, asking you whether you want to sign up for a newsletter that sends recommendations on crime thrillers, or romance, or non-fiction, most blogs will have a single genre focus and feature archived postings that are designed to be read. Unlike book promotion sites, which focus on showing you what's being promoted right-this-second, blogs tend to have more in-depth and personalized reviews of books that are featured. A lot of book blogs have Op/Eds, fluff pieces, and other kinds of articles that have nothing to do with book reviews.

HOW BLOGGERS MAKE MONEY

For some bloggers, posting book reviews and features is simply a labor of love, or at least a labor of breaking even. Running a nice blog takes an unbelievable amount of time—there are logos to develop, stock art to buy, web hosting and domain names to pay for, social media assets to maintain and—oh, yeah—you've got to read the books you're talking about and drum up your own readers to follow your blog. Smaller-time bloggers do alright recouping their costs and even making a little money from affiliate programs like Amazon Associates. They're committed to talking about books they love, and they're generally not making a killing or charging for paid placements.

Big bloggers are different. They've worked hard to build

enormous followings on their web pages, newsletters, and on social media. They've established themselves as experts in everything that has to do with their category. They're some hybrid between the book promotion sites and small-time bloggers. They're not just in business to make money like the book promotion sites are, but they're committed to the publishing world and to books. Blogs like this (let's call them "big romance blogs") do charge for placement.

Similar to book promotion sites, prices and results will vary. Heroes and Heartbreakers, for example, doesn't have a single ad unit under $300. A look at some of the more comprehensive packages will quickly get you into the $800 range. The pricing models of some of the larger blogs recall older advertising world standards. Placements may be pricey, but stacked placements (your ad appearing in more than one spot on the page), runs and exposure may also be longer.

On the other end of the pricing spectrum are what I would call growth-bloggers—those who have built a dedicated enough base that they can charge for direct advertising placements in order to build more profitable blogs. You won't be hard-pressed to find some very nice-looking blogs offering the same ad package Heroes and Heartbreakers does for a hell of a lot less money. To name just one, Smart Bitches Trashy Books has a very strong brand, an impressive social media followership, and really great pricing on its ads.

WHAT IT TAKES TO BUY DIRECT PLACEMENT ADS ON BLOGS

There are two kinds of ad placements you're likely to find on a blog. In some cases, you'll be able to buy what's called a sponsored story. In this kind of placement, the blogger will be writing an article about you that looks like a standard posting but that you've actually paid for. For example, a blogger might do mostly unpaid book reviews but sell spots for "book reviews" (wink,

wink) that are really advertisements. They are designed in such a way to let content about you or your book blend in with other content that is organic. This could also be true for an author interview-type posting. Spots like this are valuable because blog followers trust the leadership of the blog and are likely to trust recommendations they find there.

Blogs may also offer placements for what the industry calls display advertising. These are graphic ads (usually banners) that appear in prominent spaces on the page. Usually, these ads are at the very top of a page near the header and/or on the right sidebar of a page. Traditionally, these ads were priced on a CPM basis (cost per 1,000 impressions). Prices that authors balk at from the bigger blogs are far lower than premium ad inventory in other sectors. These blogs are skewing to market—realizing that many authors and publishers can't afford or won't pay CPMs like these, and with high-performing promo sites in the mix, pricing has become increasingly arbitrary.

The technical capabilities you'll need for a sponsored placement aren't intimidating. For a sponsored book review or interview you may be asked to provide a sample of the book or be asked a series of preparatory questions. Display ads are a different story. In this case, you have to pony up an actual ad. Usually this means supplying a graphic asset in a standard ad size and format—728x90 and 300x250 pixels are among the most popular sizes. Additional specs may vary. Animated gifs can be smart. Depending on how sophisticated the blog is, you may need one that's DoubleClick compliant. The better the ad, the more books you'll sell. Unless you're a Photoshop ninja with ad design experience, hire a pro.

CHOOSING PAID BLOG PLACEMENTS

I know you want me to name names. Believe me, I'm not trying to skimp on giving you real examples of blogs that are friendly to steamy romance. But this is a static book, and over time, things will change. Blogs that are here today are gone tomorrow and they can be a bit flakier than book promotion sites about their pricing, products and plan. For that reason, I'll refer you to the Marketing Steamy Romance website for the most extensive, and current, listings.

OTHER NICHE ADVERTISING OPPORTUNITIES

For the sake of completeness, I want to mention a few more niche channels where authors of erotic romance at least have the opportunity to peddle their wares. A goal of this book is to broadly expose the set of arenas where authors of steamy books are allowed to play. My own marketing preferences skew toward competitively priced, focused, measurable digital opportunities. Not all the tactics presented below are ones that I have, or plan to, try. They are right for some authors and in this section I'll do my best to present a balanced summary of the pros and cons of each so you can decide whether they're right for you.

TRADE PUBLICATIONS

Organizations with strong ties to the greater industry, such as Romantic Times and Romance Writers of America(RWA) offer ads for print and digital channels. These are large organizations that host conferences, maintain websites, send newsletters, and whose tentacles reach far in terms of getting to readers and industry pros. They know that steamy and erotic romance are important sub-genres of the romance category and their ad products are friendly to authors of erotic fiction. Like some of the bigger blogs, their pricing is more aligned with older advertising models. Advertising in trade publications doesn't come cheap. Yet, the people who follow them are extraordinarily committed to the romance genre. Many of their readers and followers love romance well enough to attend their annual mega-conferences. As a result, publications like this often feature special issues and placement opportunities related to key events.

CONFERENCES, BOOK SIGNINGS AND READER EVENTS

Beyond conferences that attract readers, other reader-focused events such as book-signings and expos are another way to gain exposure. Voracious readers love to meet their favorite authors and can have a bit of hero worship when it comes to meeting any authors at all. Contrary to what some of our royalties may indicate, a whole lot of people out there really appreciate what we do!

First and foremost, these events are *fun*. The exception may be if you're introverted and terrified by crowds. If you're anything like me, you find writing isolating and get giddy any time you get to interact with actual people. I'll admit it — I love everything about in-person events. For me, it doesn't get any better than going out for adult beverages every night and hanging out with people of the non-tiny variety who don't expect me to feed them and won't put cheddar Goldfish in my hair.

Event screening is important. The bigger ones can be really expensive to participate in. The RT Convention and RWA Conference charge in the neighborhood of $500 each. That doesn't include whatever you might pay to have a table. In their defense, they are industry conferences that offer a lot in terms of networking and professional development. Standalone book signings and reader events are cheaper, but the smaller ones also attract smaller crowds. Smaller crowds may not be a bad thing. Mega-events can be overwhelming. Better conversations can be had and more meaningful relationships built when there's not such a frenetic vibe.

Some younger and smaller author events have been exposed as scams. I've heard of a couple of cases where an organizer drummed up authors for an event that was never intended to happen. More often, I've seen what I believe to be organizers who are in over their heads. Organizers typically collect author registration fees well in advance but may find that they can't pull the event off. Maybe it's undersubscribed (whether by authors or readers) and they have to call it off. I've heard of events being canceled and authors having a hard time getting their money back. This is where research comes in. Really check out the people you're dealing with and think critically about what you stand to get from this kind of event. If the big anchor authors who have signed on barely resemble what you right, you're unlikely to get a great return on investment.

And, about that ROI...if it's not local, you have to pay to get there, pay for a hotel, pay a fee to host a table, and even pay to have your books and swag shipped so you have inventory to sell. The ROI on paperbacks might be pretty high. I can buy most of my paperbacks from the printer for $3 to $5 apiece. If I sell them at list price ($6.99 for the novellas and $12.99 for novels) I'm doing better than I would for an eBook. At that rate, however, I'd still need to sell more than 100 books to even make $500. If I paid a conservative $1,500 just getting to the conference, I'm not making back my money. No one I know sells anywhere close to that at conferences. If nothing else, readers also have to worry about how many books they can fit in their bags.

So, as you consider opportunities such as these, think in terms of both tangible and intangible benefits and not just what you'll spend. I tend to view these conferences more as social opportunities than anything else. I go in with a hope of having fun and making friends. It's also not a bad excuse to check out a new place if the location is fun. A lot of people bring their spouses and get a little sightseeing done. Remember, it's a business expense.

CHAPTER EIGHT

AWARDS AND CONTESTS

A wards and contests may be the most underutilized advertising channel for authors of steamy romance. No other channel guarantees that anybody new will actually read your book. With awards and contests, your work will be read by judges who enjoy reading in your genre—people who love it enough to volunteer their time, and who are open to reading new authors—people who will feel like winners if judging exposed them to a well-enjoyed book.

This chapter deconstructs awards and contests—what value they stand to offer, how they work, and how to choose a set that might be a fit for you. Even if you don't think your books are award-winning quality, I'll list compelling reasons to consider adding the right awards and contests to your marketing ecosystem. From the benefits of finaling, to the provision of scorecards, to the ability to gauge the competition, other value can often be found here, whether you win or not.

A STRONG CASE FOR ENTERING AWARDS

Here, I'll refer to an award as a competition that deals primarily in completed and released works. If you wrote something wonderful, putting it out on the right awards circuit is a solid strategy for gaining recognition. By "the right awards circuit", I mean the set of awards that is legitimate, aligned to your writing level or career stature, and sized correctly for you to be able to place or win. This list details what benefits you can expect, depending on how far you get.

- **JUDGES WHO BECOME READERS.** First round judges are nearly always unpaid volunteers who offer to score books in genres they love. They are voracious readers who may be on the hook to judge three or more entries. These are people who want good fiction to be recognized, who are eager to discover new authors, and who will keep reading your books if they liked the one they judged. They may even do you the courtesy of writing a public review, on their own time, for your published book. I myself have experienced this fan/follow effect both as a judge and as a judged author.
- **INFLUENTIAL PLAYERS WHO LEARN YOUR NAME.** Awards organizations dangle influential editors, agents, and publishing-world talent in front of authors, appealing to their aspirations to be more widely-recognized and more in demand. Utilized as final round judges, these influencers are motivated to understand what books first round judges rallied around in order to gauge the marketplace and gain access to new talent. Authors are also attracted to matchmaking possibilities. An indie author who wants to be traditionally-published may get her foot in the door with a big deal editor. A traditionally-published

author who's ready for a step up may get in with a better agent who has fresh ideas around how to sell her books.

- **A RESUME-BOOSTER IF YOU FINAL.** Making it to the finals, even if you don't win, still earns you credibility that you can leverage. *Snapdragon*, was a Semi-finalist in the Publisher's Weekly BookLife Prize for Fiction, a point I can mention from now until the end of time. I blogged about it. I put the articles announcing the Quarterfinalists and Semi-finalists on my web site's media page. I added it to the book synopsis page on my web site and posted it to my social media accounts. I placed a note about it, including a judge's quote, under the Editorial Reviews on my Amazon page. I wrote ad copy that alluded to it—my ads that mentioned this recognition did twice as well as ads that didn't. And any time I pitch an agent or editor this year you can bet I'll mention the honor.
- **MEDIA COVERAGE IF IT'S A BIG AWARD.** It won't hurt to have your name in the news. Being mentioned in conjunction with a well-publicized award amounts to free promotion for your book. Tens of thousands of prospective new readers will read your name if coverage is on a national scale. Some awards organizers pay to advertise the winners on visible sites, including the RWA magazine or the RT Book Reviews web site.
- **NETWORKING IF THERE'S A CEREMONY.** Some of the bigger awards have large, formal ceremonies that offer VIP treatment to finalists. If you've been invited to attend the ceremony, chances are you'll also be invited to some sort of private reception. Also on the invite list will be the judges affiliated with the contest and publishing pros interested in meeting promising new talent.

- **IRREVOCABLE "AWARD-WINNING" STATUS IF YOU WIN.** That's right. If you win an award, you get to repeat that you're an award-winning author. And if your book wins an award, you get to repeat that it's an award-winning book. Depending on the award, there may be a seal, symbol, or foil that you can place on the cover to show the book's distinction. These symbols serve as immediate, and highly positive, visual cues to readers, and will only help your sales.
- **A SYMBOLIC MEMENTO AND/OR AN ACTUAL PRIZE WITH MONETARY VALUE.** Depending on the award, you may win something of monetary value. Hopefully, this is actual money; but it could also be services authors buy (e.g., editing, design services, free advertising) or some other perk (e.g., travel and entry to an industry event). Other priceless awards may be advertised as prizes, such as a meeting with an industry bigwig or a commitment for a bestselling author to blurb your book. At absolute least, you'll end up with some physical certificate or award. Even without the fanfare and pageantry of a major award, this type of recognition will feel good.

SHOULD YOU ENTER?

I know what you're thinking: those benefits sound great as long as you final or win. But don't give up yet! Even if your book is *not* wonderful, you still have a shot. That's because awards are numbers games. Your book won't succeed or fail based on how good it is in any absolute sense—all it has to do is score better than other entries.

On a scale of one to ten, your book may be a tepid seven, but if everyone else who entered was a sex, guess what? You win! I know this sounds crazy. The reality is, many organizers don't do much hustling to promote their awards. Poorly-advertised competitions end up with few entrants. And I'll tell you a secret: a lot of multi-genre awards have struggled to attract erotic romance entrants. Some organizers have dropped the erotic category altogether.

On the opposite end of the spectrum are oversubscribed awards. Some of the bigger ones in the romance category, such as the RITAs, cap entries to a certain number and tend to reach their maximums within the first day. If you want to get a sense for how competitive various awards are, and to determine whether a specific award is a good fit for your books and your brand, scrutinize clues such as these as you peruse the web site and read the rules.

- HOW SIMILAR ARE THE BASIC CIRCUMSTANCES OF YOU AND YOUR BOOKS TO THE AUTHORS AND BOOKS THAT WON LAST YEAR? If everyone who won last year was a bestselling author with ten books under her belt and a long history of writing cookie-cutter steam with major houses, think twice if you are a debut indie author who's written something avant garde. Chances are, most people who judge that contest really like the kinds of books that have won. If you think you've written the breakthrough novel that the contest doesn't know it's looking for, by all means: *enter it*. But be prepared for the possibility that even a book that is a superior piece of literature may not make the cut if it's simply a bad fit for the award.
- HOW GOOD ARE THE BOOKS THAT WON LAST YEAR COMPARED TO YOURS? I know, I know. Good is subjective. Like, *really* subjective. But it's not going to hurt to go to Amazon and download samples of the top three books that placed in your category last year. If nothing else, it will give you a sense for the level of editorial quality the judges were looking for. If you look at all three finalists together, you'll know whether

the final round judge's pick was closest to what she buys or sells, or whether it was less personal to what she may have favored.

- WHO ARE THE FINAL ROUND JUDGES? Along those lines, check out the final round judges. Judges are used to getting excited about books in the genre and style they buy in, or in that of the kinds of authors they represent. If your work isn't a great fit for final round judges, you may want to pass on the award.

- DO ENTRIES OPEN AT A SPECIFIC TIME OF DAY? An award web site that takes electronic entries and that specifies day, time and time zone is probably expecting a lot of entries. An award that people know about—and care about—enough to enter the second it opens may be highly competitive.

- IS A FINITE NUMBER OF ENTRIES SPECIFIED AND/OR IS IT POSSIBLE THAT THE AWARD WILL CLOSE BEFORE THE ENTRY DEADLINE IF IT MAXES OUT? This is another signal that organizers are expecting a lot of entries and that the award may be heavily-entered and well-known.

- HAS THE DEADLINE BEEN EXTENDED? On the other hand, extensions can be a signal that awards organizers are hoping for more entries. Nobody wants the administrative burden (nor the loss of face) to cancel an award because it is undersubscribed, especially if the award is tied to the organizer's reputation or a tradition.

BEST FIRST BOOK AWARDS

Let's be honest: big authors have an advantage. Their books have been edited by industry veterans. Their covers have been professionally designed, and if they're traditionally published, they already have at least some of what industry pros (read: judges) are looking for. If you are a debut author, awards season has something you'll want to get in on: many competitions have "Best First Book" awards. These offer a great opportunity to gain recognition for your work on a playing field that is a bit more level. And it's a great way to have a shot in larger competitions.

AVOIDING BAD OUTCOMES

SHAMELESS PROFITEERING. Not all awards are created equally. Some have close ties to writer and reader communities. Others...well, let's just say they don't. Beware of trumped-up competitions with tenuous ties to the publishing community. Organizers of awards such as this often feature a long list of categories (to increase their revenue potential) and charge inexplicably lofty fees. Most award organizers are looking to make a little money. Certainly, there are legitimate administrative and advertising expenses that have to be covered through entry fees. In some cases, high-profile judges may be paid an honorarium to judge. But if the organizers are charging bucketloads of money just to enter, advertising widely, and the benefits to finalists and winners aren't that sweet, move on and find a better competition.

One clear red flag to me is when I see awards that only accept ebooks charging in the high two-figure and low three-figures per entry. It's one thing if award organizers ask for paperbacks and charge fees that cover their costs for distributing those paperbacks to judges. But when the logistics of distributing entries to judges aren't complex, where is that money going?

The best way to weed out scammers is to be a good detective. Look at past winners to see whether gaining recognition seemed to give them a lift. If the book they won the award for is struggling in sales and reviews, you can be sure the award-win didn't do much, supposing the award win was recent. Google the names of winning authors along with the name of the award. Look at the award organizer's online presence and social media following. Do they appear well-networked with readers or industry people?

Apart from awards season, are those in their audience engaged? Will you get score cards or feedback on your entry? Be vigilant in scrutinizing any organizer that has the audacity to ask for three-figure entry fees.

BOOK DYSMORPHIA. You think your book is amazing. What makes you believe this? What are your average reviews? If you write series, how are the sales for books beyond the first in line? And don't forget the friend discount. If you have fifty reviews and thirty of them are from people you know, at least thirty of those reviews are from people with mixed incentives for being honest with you. Looking only at strangers' reviews, how much harder were they in their assessments? Did they seem like literary connoisseurs who knew a thing or two about the art of story craft, or did their expectations seem a bit lower? If you're not confident that your book has a shot based on quality alone, choose awards that offer scorecards. Especially if you have these sorts of doubts about your book, candid feedback from judges is a good perk.

CONTESTS

Contests are like awards, except they tend to be for unpublished works. In place of recognizing recent titles for excellence in their category, the goal may be to discover the next hot author or the next hot book. Some contests ask for a completed manuscript, but many ask instead for an excerpt. I've seen contests that focus on everything from the first three pages, to the first 5,000 words, to the final chapter, to the synopsis. Contests such as these are looking toward a critical element to serve as the barometer for the overall quality and market potential of the book.

The most attractive among these offer hard commitments to

the winner, the holy grail being a contract to buy the manuscript. Often, finalists will be asked to supply a full manuscript somewhere along the way. As with awards, contests such as these carry benefits for authors whose work is strong enough to get noticed within the process. Entrants may earn new readers through the process of being judged. The names of finalists will be known and their work will be seen by industry pros.

Contests also have a greater focus on providing feedback to entrants. Some contests are open to unpublished manuscripts, but an entire universe caters to unpublished authors. It is common to offer first round scorecards as feedback to authors. Some contests go beyond numerical scores and offer any accompanying commentary the reviewer provided—a pretty sweet perk! Particularly for an unpublished work, scores will be an indicator of your entry's strengths and weaknesses, and how well it might do if pitched to editors and agents.

As with awards, the cost vs. benefit of entering has to be considered. Compared to awards, contest entry fees tend to be more modest. Still, it's important to understand how well the contest aligns to your proficiency level and career status compared to other entrants—especially if you care a lot about your entry being seen in the finals, or your chances at a win. Also, scan judge lists and think about who you're targeting. If an editor at the publishing house you've been trying to get attention from is a final round judge, by all means, enter! Awards and contests are ideal for strong writers who simply need their foot in the door. If that's your situation, it will behoove you to engage so you can get noticed.

Finally, consider doing what I do: viewing contests that return scorecards as a paid feedback mechanism. I don't care if I blow $30 on a contest if I know that I'll see the scorecards from three judges, whether I make it to the finals or not. In that case, I will have paid only $10 per opinion on my excerpt and maybe even my manuscript—opinions from somebody completely impartial who was eager to read my entry and to judge.

One of my favorite pieces of advice for rising authors working on their craft is to enter contests won by authors much bigger or much different from them, and to see how their scores stack up. Adopting this "smaller fish in a bigger pond" approach will tell you whether you're in their league or whether you have a lot of work to do.

WHEN YOU WIN (OR DON'T WIN)

WHEN YOU GET BAD SCORES. Bad scores—just like bad reviews—are a blessing. No writer ever got better from everybody loving his work. If you've entered a contest or put in for an award that offers scorecards, even if you don't final, you will be shown the strengths and weaknesses of your books. In a best case scenario, judge scores will be consistent. Look for patterns and know that where you universally scored high or low is where you can be sure of weaknesses and strengths. Sometimes there will be less alignment between what judges had to say. I tend to think that if three different people felt differently about what they loved or hated, the emotional responses you're trying to cultivate within your reader might not have come through clearly enough in your book.

While reader reviews can be taken with a grain of salt, I wouldn't be too dismissive of contest scores. Every once in awhile, you'll get a judge who simply doesn't understand you or your writing. In general, the feedback of peers who know something about story craft and writing books that can sell is something that shouldn't be ignored.

WHEN YOU FINAL, BUT DON'T WIN. Let's get something straight: a final is a win. Winning is nice, but your real goal is to get far enough to claim bragging rights. If you're looking for an agent or publisher, or for a better agent or a better publisher, award nods will be another notch on your belt. The first thing to do is promote your success—even if the competition isn't over. Write a blog post about making it however far you've come. Develop ads that talk about your status. Post it on social media. Put it in your newsletter. You'll gain new readers from it, and your current readers will be happy to have discovered you early, and to ride the sparks of your star.

WHEN YOU WIN. Keep bragging. Shout it from the mountaintops. Re-post any free promotion you get from it and boost your success on social media. Revise your book descriptions on online retail pages to let readers know about your win. Post a video on your YouTube channel. Reach out to important blogs and ask them to interview you about the book that won. And, back to agents and editors: if you've won an award, pitch the hell out of whatever you're working on and make sure everyone knows about your recent success. Winning an award is validation that people who know what they're talking about loved your book. Agents and editors will be interested in anyone who has the chops to make future books sell.

CHAPTER NINE

INFLUENCER TACTICS

An influencer is simply someone with the clout to make other people take action. When a strong influencer tells her audience to jump, they ask "how high?" Every tactic that's been discussed so far deals in the currency of influence to a certain extent. This chapter explores professional services and other opportunities that use influence in more obvious or aggressive ways.

There is only one rule to evaluating channels discussed in this chapter: screen based on their ability to cultivate action among your perfectly-aligned target base. Anyone who has access to the kinds of readers who will love your books, a microphone to make sure they get the message, and a track record of engagement is someone you should consider adding to your team. Not all influencers will get in bed with just any author, or allow themselves to be taken to bed at all. The kinds of influencers mentioned in this chapter are ones who are open to being approached and who may earn a living from using their sway.

PROMOTERS AND PERSONAL ASSISTANTS

Promoters in this genre give themselves all kinds of names and theirs can run the gamut of services. I'll use the terms "promoter" and "personal assistant", or PA, interchangeably to describe a person who spends time on your behalf rallying readers to discover your books. When we usually think of PAs, we think of administrative skills. The role promoters play certainly include those. Yet, a good PA brings value to the table that goes far beyond administration. The best ones have their own engaged set of followers.

What will a promoter do for you? She will coordinate street teams and ARCs. She will organize events, such as release parties for your books. She'll drum up authors to do takeovers on your page and entice as many readers as possible to attend. She'll blast out broadcasts to let everyone in her audience know about any timely news that relates to you.

Full-service PAs also coordinate other sorts of promotions and anything else that has to do with the amplification of your brand. She may be deeply entrenched in your business, posting on social media on your behalf, arranging newsletter swaps and other promos, and acting as your proxy in certain settings, as when you're invited to do other author takeovers. Even if you think you need more of an assistant to act on your behalf, don't underestimate the value of having a team member who will externally validate your work by hyping you through her own profile.

My Facebook feed is full of authors looking for referrals for a "great" PA. But a PA who gets amazing results for paranormal authors may not be the one for you if what you need are readers of dark romance. Your goal is to find new readers. You should be looking for PAs with large, engaged followerships who trust their advice and take action with respect to books in your niche.

One bad strategy I see is hiring a PA whose influence has too much overlap with your network. Beware of PAs with whom you have scores of friends in common—if the only people they can reach are people who you can reach, they are too close within your orbit. Don't let your desire for someone who's been vetted by people you know to outweigh your own critical thinking on who's a good fit. A PA whose audience simply doesn't align with yours will not yield optimal results.

In terms of strategy, the more the merrier. My view of working with PAs is that you don't have to limit yourself to only one. If you can afford ten PAs, each of who has a different set of followers who read your genre, hire them all and place one in charge of coordinating the others. It is common for more than one PA to promote the same set of events in support of a single author. Their scope of influence is, in many ways, far more valuable than how they can contribute to alleviating the burden of administrative tasks.

BLOGGERS

Back in the olden days, when bloggers had no shot at making money, they were honest to goodness influencers. I know I've talked about bloggers in the context of selling ads and making money through affiliate programs. There are plenty of bloggers who decidedly do *not* take money, but who have huge followings and review a lot of books. Looking for bloggers who could influence readers to buy your book is a strategy you should be pursuing. Yet, the same basic principle that is true for PAs is true for bloggers. Looking for some blogger—*any* blogger—to review your book is not a great approach.

I made the mistake of looking for the biggest bloggers I could find to cover my debut novel. I was thrilled when a mega-blogger with a lot of clout agreed to take it on. Counter to my hopes, she flamed my book because she didn't like my hero—she gave it its very first three-star review. For weeks, I was convinced that it was she who made a mistake. My book was beautifully written— most of my other reviews were five stars and my book was doing well elsewhere on the circuit. What I hadn't seen clearly was that her blog was full of five-star reviews for books with alpha heroes with less complex setups than mine. I'd sent her a book that was never going to be her cup of tea. Bloggers—just like reviewers—will ding a good book if it's not what they usually read. In expecting a great review for a book that was wrong for the reviewer and the audience, the mistake had been all mine.

Even a great review won't do you any favors if the blog is a bad fit. Look beyond sub-genres and tropes to find out what the readers are truly open to. This is especially true for heat level. If you're interested in finding paying readers, don't waste your time with bloggers who post a lot of deals and freebies. If the blog caters to binge readers and high volume authors, walk away if you don't have a huge library to keep them hooked on you.

CRITICAL REVIEWS

Look no farther than the internets to find all sorts of opinions on whether professional reviews are bullshit. Be assured that if money were no object, no sensible author would turn down a positive critical review. The most influential critical reviews are editorial. Think the New York Times book review and RT reviews: you couldn't buy one if you tried. Sometimes PR agents with journalist relationships grease the wheels for placements like these.

More commonly, authors wanting critical feedback can simply pay for a professional review. The intention behind them is legitimate enough. So is the basic logic: that an impartial person with literary chops is in the best position to comment on a book's quality; and that because reading books takes time, fees cover administrative and labor costs. But there are fees and then there are *fees*. Some of the more influential critical review services charge as much as $500 and return notes that read more like book summaries than critiques. You can buy critical reviews for a lot less but reasonable prices are typically from players who may be in it for the money, with fewer real publishing world ties and without much clout.

My personal opinion is that many of these services aren't worth it for any author. The quality of reviews I've read (even for my own books) has rarely been worth the money paid. They take a long time to come back (sometimes six to eight weeks) and if you want critical reviews before a book launch, you need to be willing to sit on your manuscript for months. RT is an outlier in that it is an unpaid service that has tons of influence and that may not choose to critique your book. Finished manuscripts must be submitted to RT four full months before the date of your book's release.

With that said, I think that critical reviews are doubly risky for authors of steamy romance. These services claim only to use reviewers with literary qualifications—they don't even pretend that if you submit a romance your book will be read by anyone with romance chops. And, trust me—I've read reviews that have made me call even basic qualifications into question. To someone who doesn't read in erotic genres, and who might not even respect it as literature, any steamy romance is unlikely to fare well.

PUBLIC RELATIONS

Traditional Public Relations agencies are focused on the customer awareness and public reputations of the brands they represent. For product-driven brands, PR campaigns seek media coverage designed to boost sales. When they're well-executed, PR campaigns yield large-scale placements that drive business results and improve brand perception.

Scale-oriented goals have certain limitations for authors of steamy books. Because of the heat level of our books, media outlets that work with other publishing genres may not cover erotic romance. That doesn't mean our books wouldn't be great for niche publications with brands in gloriously irreverent alignment to the kinds of books we write. Forget The Washington Post—get a writer from Jezebel or Bustle to rave about your book.

Because it is expensive to hire a PR agency, they tend to be hired by publishers or indie authors who are doing well. Though it's possible to see huge sales from a single, great media spot, PR tactics don't typically show a clear return on investment. Running a PR agency is a relationship-based business. An agency's incentives lie with dazzling the mega-influencers of romance readers they rely on for coverage. No agency wants to alienate a mega-influencer like USA Today Happy Ever After. For that reason, PR agencies avoid representing mediocre authors who would force them to lose credibility with their network for hawking terrible books.

Consequently, reputable PR agencies are willing to take on solid authors with good books featuring tropes that are trending in the markets. In this sense, they work like traditional publishers—they good ones are scrutinizing prospective authors and looking for those whose work can sell. Taking on authors who are a sure thing also makes sense for their client relationships. Because they are expensive, clients expect big results. There are some exceptions here when it comes to large publishers, who may have big accounts with big agencies that have the ability to sway mega-influencers to promote whatever they want.

I made the mistake of deciding on PR as a critical element of my launch plan for my first novel. As a marketer who had spent some ten years working in agencies by that point, I had seen PR work for many brands. I loved my book's story, was convinced that I brought something new and different to the market, and just knew that journalists would want to interview me. My PR agent got me an interview on USA Today's Happy Ever After blog and a guest blog spot on Heroes and Heartbreakers. Ever After Romance featured an exclusive excerpt of my book. I love the fact that this coverage lends credibility to my brand on my media page. But if I knew then what I know now about book marketing, I could have spent the same money and gotten 2,500 new readers to buy my book.

And mine was a reputable PR agent who I had worked with on other projects and who had some pretty sick chops in the publishing world. It wasn't that she failed to get the kind of coverage I could reasonably expect for an author of my (then-nonexistent) career status. It was that I had overestimated the role that PR could play in earning me new readers for my book.

Consider PR only if you have the money, only if you really have a killer story angle or author brand, and only if you can trust the agent or agency. This, you can sniff out by looking for clear relationships with industry journalists and a track record of helping authors like you. Be realistic about what it's designed to do compared to other tactics (to place more credibility around your brand and make you seem like an important author—not necessarily to yield an immediate or direct jump in sales).

CHAPTER TEN

UNIQUE AND CREATIVE OPPORTUNITIES

A final set of channels that can dig up new readers will be discussed in this chapter. Because authors of erotic romance have diminished access to traditional channels, tactics like these help us make up for some of the disadvantage. I'm a lover of innovative solutions and creative ways to expand our reach. If you have other obscure tactics that are less common or less direct in terms of earning new readers, e-mail me. I want to hear about them.

SECONDARY RETAILERS

Secondary retailers, such as Excitica and Blushing Books, allow published authors to list their titles. Their sole focus is on steamy and erotic books, and they don't charge upfront fees for listing. Like most retailers, their revenue model is to collect fees before giving you your royalties.

Yet, they are not exactly like the Amazons and Smashwords of the world. Their processes aren't automated. There's no filling in a web form, and, boom! You're done. You'll have to submit an application, wait to hear back, and sign a legal contract specifying terms and royalties.

One drawback of services such as these is that your manuscripts may be offered as downloads. For those of us who go nuts to think about pirating, this can induce a bit of angst. Be resigned to the fact that if you put your work out there on some of these sites, it's out there. It's more like selling on Smashwords (which also lets users download if they buy your books directly and if you have that option chosen) than on a site that cracks down on digital rights. There's no protected, dynamic delivery of your book to an ereader as you would find on Amazon, Barnes & Noble or Apple with Kindle, Nook or iBooks.

I won't pass a value judgment on whether you should use sites such as these. Depending on the site, the branding can be lower quality. Some of them have nice-looking websites with books that seem professional and polished while others don't seem curated or choosy at all. That could be an advantage to any author whose assets look more professional. If your cover is great and your book is well-rated, they may jump on the chance to make your book more visible.

KINDLE SCOUT AND KINDLE WORLDS

One way smart authors are making good money at selling books and earning new readers is through participation in Kindle Worlds and Kindle Scout. Because it's Amazon, there are requirements around limiting your digital versions to Kindle. If that wouldn't alienate too many of your readers, here are some reasons why you might want to join in.

KINDLE WORLDS. Kindle Worlds lets readers write stories that align to established franchises—typically current, popular movies, television shows and books. If you're confused, think fan fiction. You get to write stories with borrowed characters and publish them on the Amazon website. Only, not every franchise is available. You have to be willing to write stories for a franchise that is licensed for the platform—ones like *Pretty Little Liars*, *The 100*, and *The Vampire Diaries*, to name a few. The goal here is to find new readers, and the idea is that if a reader discovers you on Kindle Worlds and simply enjoys your writing, he will check out your original fiction.

In order to play in this space, you have to actually know the franchise, or be willing to go read a book series or watch a show from start to finish to craft a story for that particular world. The bigger challenge may be finding something in your genre. You may love *The Vampire Diaries*, but if your author brand isn't about vampires, writing in Kindle Worlds for that franchise is liable to confuse the hell out of your readers.

Still, there's real opportunity here. You may have a story with a hero and heroine (or a hero and hero or a heroine and heroine...I'm not one to judge) whose character archetypes fit the archetypes of characters in a Kindle Worlds franchised book or show. In that case, if you're willing to kiss goodbye the idea of ever publishing that story as an original fiction, you could rework it in order to expose yourself to new readers and take advantage of the Kindle Worlds boost. Since you're writing stories for licensed franchises, the rights you retain to what you've written are very different from that of traditional books.

This may be a better solution for authors of teapot-level steam than it is for those who write hotter stuff, though each world has its own rules, and some are quite permissive. Language from Fiona Davenport's world, *Passion, Vows and Babies* has content guidelines that mention "Craft Romance with Intention" as allowed, saying that "Sexual content (including erotica) is permitted, but we don't accept pornography or offensive depictions of graphic sexual acts." If there's a franchise you love, or are willing to love, give it a try.

KINDLE SCOUT. Kindle Scout allows authors to enter their uncontracted, unpublished original fiction into sort of a contest in which prospective readers have to vote. If enough readers upvote your book during the 30-day promotion period, Amazon gives you a $1,000 advance and a publishing contract for your book.

If it wouldn't alienate too many of your readers who buy outside of Amazon, this route has some pretty sweet perks. Anyone who voted for your book will get it for free if you're among those selected for a contract. While under contract with Amazon, your backers will be the first to receive your book and will be permitted to leave ratings before the official release date. As your publisher, they will work to give your book visibility. With an advance paid to you and skin in the game, they will be invested in seeing your book succeed. In this game, if Amazon wants you to succeed, you win.

Kindle Scout features romance categories, and plenty of its books have heat, including behind closed doors sex scenes. I'll admit that I've never seen a fetish lifestyle book on Scout, but that doesn't mean there hasn't been one. If they accept your manuscript (and they don't accept all of them), you've got a shot.

PART THREE

COVERING YOUR ASS

CHAPTER ELEVEN

A BRIEF NOTE ON ASS-COVERING

B efore I dive into strategies of getting yourself out of hot water if you find yourself in the boiling pot, I'll underscore a few things you can do to stay out of trouble altogether. I know what the common wisdom says: *just get yourself out there*. The myth that authors are successful because their books are everywhere is a damaging lie. Believe me—avoiding persnickety complainers who will only kvetch about the offensive nature of your content is a blessing in disguise. The sooner you can weed out people who aren't going to buy your book, and who may even be hostile to the very idea of your genre, the better.

This concept prescribes a need to keep tight control of what you're putting out there. One of my very well-meaning PAs posted some pretty graphic pages from one of my books. She was pulling the lever she knew how to pull in order to lure readers who like the good stuff. But it could have led to costly ramifications to my brand. I know it's frustrating. We all see images and copy and all other manner of racy content that would convince you that anything goes. It's simply not true, and in jail with one of the big gatekeepers is not where you want to be. Be judicious in what you're willing to post publicly, and save the racier stuff to focused audiences who'll appreciate the representation of your brand.

Beyond brand-killers and exposure-killers, profit-killers lie in wait. Don't blame all your problems on gatekeepers and their evil plans to keep hot sex in its place. Sometimes marketing fail because decisions could have been better. This final section of the book is about other actions (or lack of action) that sets authors on the road to ruin, supplying advice for all manner of covering your ass.

CHAPTER TWELVE

DEALING WITH BANS AND BLOCKS

Anything can be reported, from social media postings, to ad units, to book listings themselves. The way I believe this is dealt with is for reported content to be given a cursory glance by a human who makes a quick decision about the legitimacy of the claim. Believe me when I tell you that, if your content is reported, nobody is taking twenty minutes, or even ten, to truly investigate the merit of the complaint. If there is a long-term consequence, such as having your book de-listed or having social media profiles or accounts banned, your only option is to persist.

Gatekeepers will tell you that their policies are non-negotiable, but perseverance can make a difference if you reach a person with enough authority. Those you are dealing with aren't bad people—they've just been given bad information and it's your job to set them straight.

This is where being fact-based is doubly-important. If you want to appeal what you think is a bad decision, don't send an unfounded complaint letter—build a case. Don't be afraid to escalate your claim, or at least to ask very politely to speak with someone else. If you can't get a supervisor, ask for a consumer affairs department. If you really want to escalate it up the chain, send a letter to an executive leadership office. Point out double-standards without throwing other authors under the bus. Be professional, but get them good and sick of having to go back and forth with you.

There may also be strength in numbers and thinks to be learned from the wisdom of crowds. In January of 2017, I joined the Erotic Authors Guild, which not only helps authors of erotic literature network internally—it plays an advocacy role. To a lesser extent, for authors of erotic content, RWA also has advocacy resources and makes attorney referrals. Larger organizations such as these have knowledge and experience that can set you in the right direction, and they may be able to step in or offer to be involved.

The important thing is to not come off as a complainer who is simply breaking the rules. Just as we are used to dealing with readers who only have sour grapes because they didn't heed warnings we clearly explained, so also will gatekeepers assume that you've been reported because you didn't do a good enough job of understanding their guidelines. Demonstrate that you know the guidelines, that your work doesn't break them (or is on par with what others are doing) and do research that shows you've done your diligence. Think in terms of what a gatekeeper needs to be able to show his bosses if his decision to reverse your ban were questioned. Make it as easy as possible for your gatekeepers to honor your request.

CHAPTER THIRTEEN

WRANGLING DISGRUNTLED REVIEWERS

S o, let's talk about bad reviews, and not the kind you get because your book is bad—the kind that happen when a reader penalizes you mostly on the basis of your heat level. Even when presented with more-than-fair warnings, disgruntled readers ding books with bad ratings—a lot. Reasons range from the carelessness of not bothering to read full book descriptions to the fact that misery-loves-company grouch-types who criticize everything in their lives buy steamy romance, too. To be accurate, it's not only erotic fiction that attracts easily-annoyed reviewers. Yet, the nature of complaints about heat level or the depiction of taboos makes the fallout for erotic book authors worse.

HAVING REVIEWS REMOVED

One thing I learned from marketing products for non-author clients is that there are ways to get rid of bad reviews. Emphasis on *some*. Legitimate gripes and not-my-cup-of-tea-type ratings are likely to stick. There is recourse, however, when a point that the reviewer makes is just plain wrong, or for customer service experiences that were out of the control of the author. Retailers give leniency for incorrect or irrelevant comments that have the potential to mislead other reviewers.

For example, if you wrote a book about rose gardening, called *A Guide to Rose Gardening*, that said in its description that the focus would be—you guessed it—rose gardening, you would be within your right to dispute a review that complains of your omissions on the topic of tulips. Because it's a user error issue— and not a book quality issue—you could file an appeal and the retailer would probably take it down.

Allison Williams, an author whose blog I like, pointed to this discrepancy in a brilliant article she wrote about why authors should learn from bad reviews. When contrasting the kinds of bad reviews authors should be eager to ignore vs. the ones they shouldn't, she shows a review for the Leonardo DiCaprio movie about a scamming stockbroker, *The Wolf of Wall Street*. Next to his one star, one reviewer wrote "There were no wolves in the movie." This is exactly the sort of review that authors (in this case, filmmakers) can have taken down.

Sometimes you'll see bad reviews from readers whose paper-back arrived damaged, or who didn't receive their ebook pre-order on time. This is a delivery issue on the retailer's part—not an error of the author—and it can be disputed and taken down. Amazon in particular has a reputation for being unfavorable to authors when it comes to slashing and burning legitimate reviews while keeping really crazy ones. Even Amazon, and certainly other retailers, will act in good faith to take down reviews that clearly don't apply to the book.

Authors of steamy reads in particular stand to benefit from this. Watch out for reviews that get your details wrong. Did someone whose real gripe seems to be the well-signaled heat level of your book get the name of your heroine wrong ? File an appeal on the grounds that someone who didn't read it closely enough to know who the main character was trolling you. Retailers can be forgiving if you can shoot holes in the credibility of a reviewer by showing they weren't paying attention.

Having bad reviews removed based on a reviewer's general annoyance over an element they were warned about is not as easy, but if you are rational and fact-based in your complaint, you've got a shot at winning an appeal. Here's how I'd do this: keep copies on file of the language use in your description. Take screen shots and make sure you know the dates that any language on your description was revised. Take screen shots of any signals or warnings you placed up front, whether they're on the cover or inside the book that signals to readers what they're going to see. If you have a particularly controversial scene that some bad reviewers are mischaracterizing, create a PDF of the scene that you can send as part of the appeal. Don't tell gate-keepers the reviewer got his facts wrong—show them.

What this will reinforce, even before the retailer reviews whether to take it down, is that you're coming to them with data. Believe me, any customer service rep who finds your case in his inbox has seen it all. If you seem fact-based, it will make the reviewer seem like the crazy one (especially if the reviewer really goes on a rant). If you don't abuse the appeal process and build a good case history with the retailer, you may find that you earn greater long-term credibility.

RESPONDING TO REVIEWS

Some people say that you should never respond to reviewers— ever—no matter what. I don't necessarily agree with this rule. Your real audience for a rebuttal isn't the reviewer, it's the new reader who's considering buying your book.

For example, I had a reviewer complain that my book ended in a cliffhanger that was not a happily-ever-after, even though it was always made clear that the book was the first in a series. The response I left did not indignantly point out the reader's negli-gence. Instead, it lightly mentions that since I didn't want to write a book that was 700 pages long, I split the story into two books that, indeed, end in a HEA for the characters.

I do agree that it's a bad idea to make it a practice to respond to bad reviews, particularly if doing so runs the risk that you will sound bitter or spiteful. You'll seem petty if every bad review is met with your response. Be sparing. If you do respond to a review, kill them with kindness. Be as sweet as apple pie. Come off friendly and be the bigger person.

CHAPTER FOURTEEN

HOW TO NOT FAIL AT PAID ADVERTISING

This final chapter of advice will walk you through a few core concepts of paid advertising. I know I said this wouldn't be a book filled with general marketing advice, but I would be remiss to leave a few things unsaid. Up until this point, I've mentioned advertising rather casually, taking it as a foregone conclusion that you're indoctrinated into the wisest ways to spend your money. My intention has been to showcase paid marketing channels as an option, and to underscore that the overwhelming majority of authors who have become successful since the era of self-publishing are, indeed, using them. What I don't want to leave you with is the unrealistic notion that all of the real variables that impact the results of any paid marketing campaign don't apply to you. This section will go a bit more in-depth about budgeting and what to expect from paid marketing channels.

HOW TO THINK ABOUT ADVERTISING

Before we start talking about individual tactics, we have to talk about goals: not all advertising goals are the same. Some advertisers are focused on short-term goals, such as trending their way onto a bestseller list, or for an immediate return on the financial investment. Others take a longer-term approach by exposing themselves to new audiences and funneling new readers into their ecosystem. Each is legitimate in its own way.

Beginning advertisers can be overly-focused on seeing their investment pay off immediately. If their ad is currently running, they want to see profits *today*. Their logic reflects what most of us were taught somewhere along the lines about the concept of Return on Investment (ROI). They only view their advertising as profitable if, for every dollar they put in, they see more than a dollar come out.

Very bad wisdom takes this expectation farther, training people looking to market any product to aim for two or three dollars in return for each one they spend. After all, the time it took the author to write the book and pay to develop and/or manage ad campaigns is also a cost. Logically, you need to recoup more than just the out-of-pocket ad spend to break even.

Yet, this is an overly-linear way to think about your ad campaigns. Most authors do try paid advertising, and a lot of them get hurt by what feels like terrible performance and walk away to lick their wounds, never to try the same ad channel again. Stories we hear of mega-marketers who sell bucketloads of books and earn what sound like phenomenal profits may be real, but these success stories often understate all that had to be in place in order to get those sort of results selling thin-margin products like books.

"Ecosystem" really is the keyword here. This relates to the next chapter about getting your house in order. Readers don't read one single ad, make one single click and have your book magically appear in their mailbox. Through the course of deciding whether to buy a book, readers are exposed to numerous data points that move them toward completing, or passing, on the sale. If you want a great conversion rate, the ad has to be great. When they get to the retailer page, they have to love the cover and become more committed to buying by finding a strong blurb. The star rating has to be high, and there can't be just a few reviews if you expect an industry-leading conversion rate on your book.

This doesn't mean that you shouldn't advertise if you don't have all those things in place. But it does mean that you should calibrate your expectations. Don't let not turning a profit or seeing what feel like bad results as a sign that you've lost. Let bad performance cause you to dig deeper on what could improve performance, and read on for more advanced thinking on expectation-setting for your campaigns.

TOTAL LIFETIME VALUE

Most marketing pros think about it like this: ROI isn't about selling a product—it's about earning a customer. What matters more than the value of an individual sale is the value of an individual customer. Smart authors think about marketing in terms of selling books. Smarter authors think in terms of cultivating new readers and expanding their fan base. These smarter authors know that it's okay to lose money selling a reader book number one if the reader buys book two, book three, book four...all the way up until book x.

This strategy isn't just for authors who write series—it's for any author with more than one book, and the more books you've released, the better. You won't be everybody's cup of tea, but among readers who really like your work, you will have earned fans who buy anything you write voraciously.

In the business world, the brand that's always used as an example to demonstrate this concept is Gillette—you know, the company that makes the razors. Their ingenious strategy was to make thin margins or even lose money on selling an initial product (in their case, the handle) in order to build a longer-term revenue stream by selling a single customer dozens upon dozens of replacement blades.

For authors, this means you might want to think about your advertising plan not in terms of how much it will cost you to sell one book but what you should be willing to spend to earn royalties from many. Marketers call this Total Lifetime Value(TLV). You may spend two dollars on advertising to sell a book that only earns you one dollar in royalties, but if your average reader buys four books at the same royalty amount, the TLV of a new reader is four dollars. Cast in that light, losing money on the campaign itself is not a losing proposition, but a winning one.

The tricky part is doing the real math. And I'm not gonna lie —if you don't have a lot of books and a moderate history of data, figuring out total lifetime value will be tough. What you're looking for is a halo effect—evidence that one book sells the next, and the next, and the next. The data will be most reliable if it has some characteristics of a controlled experiment, that is, if the circumstances of your sales can be reasonably attributed to your own upselling, rather than to other promotion you're doing for certain books.

For example, if you have a series, look at the percentage of people who buy the second book, then the third. If the last book in the series teases a new book or series in the back section, how are the sales of the book or the series that was teased? What you're looking for here are sales that are not a result of advertising. So if you're advertising all of your titles at once, stop doing that for awhile. Advertise only your starter book and see how well that lends to readers buying others.

An exercise like this takes patience and may temporarily slow down some of your sales, but I've learned invaluable things by doing this with my books. I learned that 12% of people who bought my starter novel during a period in which I was promoting it bought the second book within a week and that another 6% bought the third. Those numbers doubled over the following week. I stopped advertising altogether for more than a month and saw a steady trickle of sales from secondary books come through in the following weeks.

I know there are factors that can distort the data. What about readers who one-click a book on a whim and don't get to actually reading it for another three months? What about readers who received ARCs or other freebies, who never paid for an early book in the series but purchased subsequent books? The numbers will be far from perfect, but they should give you some idea of how effective you've been at getting readers to continue reading your books.

If you've got a big enough library and you're not seeing evidence that a critical mass of readers is moving from book to book, stop advertising until you fix the bigger problem—that your starter book may not be performing. For every reader that lets books languish on his to-be-read list for weeks, there is another reader who starts reading the second he buys a book. If you sell a hundred copies of book one, on day one of a paid promotion and you haven't sold twenty-five copies of book two by day thirty of the cycle, think hard about how you can convert more readers to your second book. Low-hanging fruit could be to simply do a better job of plugging book two at the end of book one. Use better language to get readers excited about it, or choose a different preview scene. If the starter book may have quality problems, run—don't walk—to hire a great editor, and start with a developmental one. Any investment in helping your starter book perform will be money well-spent.

Finally, there may be other optimization opportunities. At the time you wrote a given book, maybe the title you teased was simply your next release. With more books written, it's possible that there's a smarter way to step people through your library. It's also an option to tease more than one book at a time—rather than stuffing your collection of books down your readers' throats chronologically, let readers choose their own adventures. Or, if you write in numerous genres, step readers through books written in genres that align to the book they just read. Be creative. The only rule is to figure out, and repeat, what works.

BRAND AWARENESS AND THE HALO EFFECT

There's something else: not all advertising is meant to have a positive ROI. Most successful brands focus at least some of their advertising dollars on brand awareness. Apple, for example, spends more than $1 Billion a year on marketing (yes—that's billion with a "B"). And most of that is on the kind of advertising that doesn't let you make an instant purchase, but that makes you feel good about the brand. When was the last time you clicked on an Apple ad and bought something from the apple store online? (Hint: the answer is never). But did you know when the most recent iPhone came out, and what made it better than earlier iPhones? (Hint: the answer is yes).

In advertising, there's something called the rule of nine that says that a consumer needs to be exposed to your brand or product at least nine times before they begin to believe in its value. Getting your name out there, even if somebody doesn't buy immediately, can have a halo effect. The halo effect is a concept that beginning advertisers aren't always comfortable with, but ask any marketer—she will tell you the halo effect is real. The basic logic is that the more a consumer sees your brand or your product, if she sees it enough times, she'll assume that everyone else knows about it, cares about it, and is buying it. Once it dawns on her that she is seeing your book everywhere, she'll conclude that the book is popular, that all her friends are reading it, and she may buy it out of a sheer fear of missing out.

I'm not telling you to launch a brand awareness campaign. Especially if you're cash-constrained, this is the last thing you should do. I don't recommend awareness tactics unless you're an experienced marketer who understands the funnel, or at least are working with one. But I do want you to be circumspect in under-standing certain immeasurable pieces of advertising campaigns. They are often working in ways that you can't yet see. I've seen many brilliant writers give up on an advertising tactic because they didn't make what they wanted to on a single campaign.

Whenever I hear an author say: "I'm not running that kind of ad again—I didn't even make my money back," I always ask them what their numbers were. Even if you didn't break even, always give the campaign credit for TLV and assume that a well-designed, well-exposed ad worked hard to solidify your brand.

And, *of course*, put on your thinking cap. I'm not saying it's a good idea to spend $100 on a tactic that only sells ten or fifteen books. The important thing is to use common sense. If you spent $60 to sell sixty books, and the book you sold leads to other books that the reader is likely to buy, you did pretty darned good.

HOW TO THINK ABOUT ADVERTISING IF YOU DON'T HAVE A LOT OF BOOKS

The math is pretty simple here. If you don't have many books to sell (yet!) the TLV of your readers is going to be low for awhile. Many readers will binge on you, but lose interest once they run out of books. Some authors mitigate this by deciding not to publish their first book until they have several in the hopper. (by the way, I think there are many compelling reasons not to do it this way, and you can read about them on my blog). The best case scenario for an author with a shallow set of books is to have a mailing list and follower on Amazon, BookBub, or some other site that notifies them of new releases.

If this is your situation, do everything you can to funnel these readers into your marketing engine so that they can feel engaged with you and be notified whenever you release a new book. This is where it becomes particularly important to build a relationship with your fan community. It's important for every author, but if you're a slow writer, or are simply at a dead end with new releases, make sure your readers feel connected to you. What you don't want is to build momentum with readers and see the relationship severed when your well runs dry. If you're never going to be the kind of author who turns out a book every six weeks, let alone every six months, relationship marketing will be critical for you.

TIMING AND TESTING

The benefits of advertising should always be seen as twofold. As an author, your primary focus will likely be on selling books. As a marketer, I care more about figuring out the repeatable model. What should matter more to you than selling books today is knowing a reliable method for selling books tomorrow, and the next day, and the next day. As you're trying different tactics, you must take measures to ensure that you're choosing conditions that make for a good test.

TIMING CONSIDERATIONS. Not all timing is equal in advertising —neither days of the week nor days of the year. Before placing an ad, buying behavior should be considered. What people buy when they're bored at work on a random Tuesday in October is different from what people buy on New Year's Day. Peoples' propensity to look for a good book around spring break (when a lot of people go on vacation or take time off because their kids are out of school) is different from their propensity to buy on a date when most people are working. And even this varies greatly from country to country.

I'm not saying that holidays are bad days—on the whole, they're not. Readers buy books who have free time. In many cases, holidays will work in your favor. One of the biggest weeks of the year for book sales is the week after Christmas (given the number of people who have just been gifted new reading devices). I'm not advising you not to advertise on special days— but I do want you to know that, from a testing perspective, days such as these are outliers.

Even outside of holidays, timing is a factor. There are entire bodies of research on the best days of the week to advertise books, and even the best times of day. *Day parting* is the name the marketing industry uses to describe strategies for the best times to serve ads. There are also better and worse days to release your book if you're trying to get it to trend and rank on important charts.

What you need to know is that if you are trying to get to a formula that you can replicate to get predictable results, you should test on a day that is similar to the kind of day you would want to run ads on over a longer term. For example, if you're looking for a platform that can earn you 100 new readers a month if you use it regularly, make choices that would let you repeat the tactic again whenever you want.

TESTING CONSIDERATIONS. Other bad logic I hear from authors is that, if an ad unit or two is not performing, the channel where the ad is being run can't work. Say you place a couple ads on Facebook. Literally, one or two, and you only show those ads to a single audience. Deciding that Facebook is a bad advertising channel if the ads tank is the wrong conclusion.

What would be true is that the ad didn't work with the audience you showed it to, and that doing well on Facebook requires you to adjust one or both. No professional marketer judges whether a channel is viable without testing variations. I've worked on projects that required me to write thirty ads for a single campaign. Depending on the scope and segmentation, a number that high may be appropriate for marketing a single book. The best-performing ad copy and imagery is crafted to fit individual audiences.

Well-crafted ads shown to well-targeted audiences will tell you a lot about what readers respond to when faced with your brand. Will you get the most clicks from an ad that mentions that your novel is award-winning? Has a five-star rating? By showing a quote from an editorial review? Maybe readers respond best to a killer tagline that alludes to your book's juicy plot. These insights have value that will pay dividends in other ways. I'm not advocating the allocation of a bottomless budget to beat messaging optimization to a pulp. Don't flush money down the toilet, but don't give up, either—not until you've learned something.

HIRING A PRO

There's a Red Adair quote I really like. It reads: "if you think it's expensive to hire a professional to do the job, wait until you hire an amateur." Mistakes cost time and money, and marketing assets that seem amateurish will not reflect positively on your brand. If you're reading this book, I know you care about marketing and are invested in doing it better. What you need to consider now is in what areas you absolutely must hire pros.

There is no one skill set that goes into marketing. Unless you're the rare unicorn who can not only author books, but also design wicked covers, write killer ads, and be robust and methodical in running ad campaigns and advertising results, you need to pick one or two lanes. If you're an author, don't sacrifice time you'd rather be spending writing taking on roles you can't be great at. It will only exhaust you and you won't get fantastic results from doing a mediocre job.

This doesn't mean you should roll up your sleeves and hustle in areas where elbow grease is all it takes. There's marketing work a trained monkey can do. If your budget is thin, it's only a matter of lending your own time to scheduling social media tweets and pimping Thunderclap campaigns. Be on Facebook and Twitter chumming it up with your readers and having fun. But don't take control of your most important assets if you can't do them justice. Unless you've been to art school, hire a cover designer. Unless you've been to writing school, hire an editor. I think you get the point.

And make no mistake—the authors who are topping the charts are marketing the hell out of their books. It doesn't matter how big you are. I see Nora Roberts, James Patterson, and Neil Gaiman books regularly in paid ad spots. This is also true for the big erotic authors. Don't believe me? Subscribe to the newsletters of some of the book promotion sites I mentioned in Part Two. Check out who's advertising on the mega-book blogs. You'll see a lot of names you recognize. You can't expect to win at a game you're not willing to play.

IF YOU THINK YOU DON'T HAVE THE MONEY

Take a minute to go back to that Red Adair quote, and think of the money not in terms of how much you're shelling out, but in terms of what *not* shelling it out will cost you. You might feel that you can't afford a price that a bona fide pro is quoting you, but consider the price of a lackluster attempt. So find the money from somewhere. And if you can't sustain the kind of money you would need to hire a particular kind of help for every book you plan to write, find the money to learn the skills to become great at it yourself.

For example, if you don't want to hire a marketing campaign manager, buy Mark Dawson's course on digital marketing. It's expensive, but spread the cost over several books and eventually it will have paid off to have learned to do it yourself. But, be brutally honest with what you're willing and able to execute and, only embark on the path of building autonomous competency if you are truly prepared to invest in the time to get it right.

IF YOU REALLY DON'T HAVE THE MONEY

An author friend of mine is legitimately broke. She lives in a country where the American dollar translates to more money than she can afford. The income levels where she lives simply don't allow her to manage the price points authors need to pay in order to play in the big arena. Her writing is brilliant, however, and she does very well based on what she's realistically able to achieve on her budget. She feels like she's failing, but given her limitations on the marketing front, she actually does quite well.

The only answer to a situation in which you literally cannot afford professional services, let alone out-of-pocket advertising spend, is to recalibrate your expectations. In the absence of being able to throw money at factors impacting the speed of your success, be prepared for a slow ascent. Speed is the variable here, but slow and steady can win the race.

The math is simple: the sooner you build your reader base, the more of each subsequent book you'll sell. If you can't boost your visibility quickly using advertising and building other assets that cost money, you can still get there, but give yourself a break. Comparing yourself to other authors who are doing better than you will kill your spirit if you don't view their success through the right lens. In a very small number of cases, a breakthrough novel sent an author to overnight stardom. But the reality is that most authors who are making a lot of money invested heavily in marketing somewhere along the way.

CHEATS AND HACKS

Many authors switch gears once they realize the difficulty of marketing. No one can say what's right for you. If you're afraid that deficiencies in your ability to do marketing well could be a career-killer, or that you simply can't make enough money as an author to justify the kind of money you would have to spend, here are some hacks that you could consider.

- **IF YOU'RE SELF-PUBLISHED, GO TRADITIONAL.** I won't pretend it's easy to get a good publishing contract. But if the idea of taking the advice in this book feels like an albatross, traditional publishing might be better-suited to you. With traditional publishing, your primary job is to sell manuscripts. If your books do well with your publisher, they'll by more. But you don't have to limit yourself to a single publisher—feel free to play the field. Many of the roles mentioned in this book, from covers, to trailers, to critical reviews and paid marketing, will be taken care of for you. You'll still have to do some brand management—you'll want a web site and active social media accounts. As I mentioned in Part II, you'll be more attractive to publishers if they look at your brand and find an engaged reader base. Particularly if you've self-published a few books, have good ratings and have a solid reader base, getting picked up by a traditional publisher may be within reach now, even if earlier attempts failed.

- **WRITE TO MARKET.** An author friend who I shall not name readily admits behind closed doors that she writes a lot of shitty books she hates. What she doesn't hate are the $12,500 a month in royalties she earns. Even as I write this, I imagine that she's home, drinking scotch and lighting her cigars with $100 bills. She has her own books that are her babies—her labors of love that she plans to publish under a different nom de plume. The books she loves to write are simply separate from the career she's built out of books that can sell. Particularly in romance, many readers care more about trending genres and tropes than they do about quality. If you can write books that readers will clamor to devour, consider it, even if it doesn't align with your artistic vision, if quitting your day job to write something—anything—is most important to you.

- **FIND A SECONDARY INCOME STREAM.** Not all authors who are making six figures are quoting their numbers based solely on the royalties they're earning from books. If you have expertise in a specific area of publishing, use higher-paid work to supplement your income in a way that lets you stay in the black. For example, I know about marketing (Duh! That's why you're reading my book). Sharing my expertise is a win for everyone involved—I add value by curating my expertise, and gain value through selling my book to an audience that wants it. If you're knowledgeable about something, you don't have to write a book, but you can become a paid blogger or speaker. Maybe you are good at cover design or editing. If you have thousands of engaged followers on social media who like your book recommendations, help other authors by becoming a PA. There's no law that says you have to make all your money from writing steamy books. If you truly are good at more than writing, *use that* and reduce the pressure on making it through royalties alone.

HOW TO HIRE PROFESSIONALS

This one is tough, and some pros are more difficult than others. Designers, for obvious reasons, are easy. Take a look at any designer's portfolio. Even if you don't know much about art theory, your gut will tell you who's good. In earlier chapters, I described how to sniff out good PR agencies and good PAs. That leaves editors and marketing campaign managers as the hardest pro team members to screen.

EDITORS. Before you hire an editor, take some time to make sure you understand the editing profession. Each time I see someone post on Facebook saying they're looking for an editor, I think to myself: what does that really mean? Developmental editors are looking for problems with the story itself—inconsistencies, unbelievabilities, and other red flags. My personal belief is that authors need access to more than one set of editing skills, and that the developmental editor has to come first.

What you'll get from these early insights is an ability to go back and "fix" your story. A developmental editor will look at plot, pacing, tension, and character to make sure the work as a whole comes together. Once you make sure the story has everything it needs, that's when it's time to bring someone in to think about line and copy edits. In my opinion, most bad reviews come down to developmental issues. Readers may not have the vocabulary to complain about flaws in the transformational arc of your character or the pacing problems your constant flashbacks presented. But, seriously—read between the lines of bad reviews. Egregious spelling mistakes and formatting issues are sometimes mentioned, but most readers aren't authorities on whether punctuation and syntax conforms to the Chicago Manual of Style. But they do understand when things about the story just don't feel right—even if they can't use the same language an editor would to understand why.

That's why putting developmental editing first is so important. You don't want to hire someone who markets himself as an editor—someone who fixes your line and copy issues—only to find that your beta readers found problems with the story itself. If that happens, you'll have to go back and fix the story, then hire someone to come through on line and copy...again. If you care about early ratings, you may even have to delay the release of your book.

Since different kinds of editors exist (I haven't even talked about line editing), the most important element to screen for is whether your prospects lead with that distinction. If you interview an editor and ask her what kind of editing she does, and she says "all of it", you might want to run. A skilled, honest editor doesn't want to stake her reputation on something she can't do well and will be candid with you about which way she leans.

That doesn't mean that editors who can do both don't exist— they absolutely do, but they can be expensive and it can be hard to get on their calendars. As you interview editors, ask about books they've edited in your genre, go read a couple of those books, and ask the author whether she'd be willing to go back into her files and share with you a few pages of the editor's marked-up copy.

A final option with editors is to ask them to do a sample edit. Pay them, of course, because editing even a chapter will require a couple hours of their time. A sample edit is also a great way to see whether feedback style and personalities fit. A friend once referred me to a big deal editor with a sterling reputation. This editor felt that I should've be honored to have even gotten a call back and willing to work with her based on reputation alone. But a good editor is a big investment. If their style of feedback isn't in a language you speak, they will still have gotten paid and you'll be left feeling like you paid for something that wasn't useful. Every author I know has had bad experiences with editors. Similarly, every editor I know has had bad experiences with authors. This is a critical relationship that really matters. So, please —*screen, screen, screen.*

MARKETING CAMPAIGN MANAGERS. Campaign managers are even more difficult to evaluate, especially if you aren't a numbers person. If you don't know what a good click-through-rate(CTR) or conversion rate is for books in your category, it will be difficult to ascertain whether any of the stats a campaign manager shares with you are good. Also, campaign managers are in the precarious position of not being able to show you all of their work. If they're ethical, they're not going to do a screen share of campaigns they're running for other authors to show you their results. Especially if you're clueless, look for campaign managers who can clearly walk you through the process. Ask them how they go about testing and optimizing campaigns, and how they would target audiences and ads that might fit for you.

Also, try to get a sense for whether they have greater

strengths around campaign optimization or building creative assets. The mix of creative and analytical skills requires use of both sides of the brain. It may be that you hire one person to develop great ads and another to run campaigns. Indeed, in a marketing agency these would be different functions. Try to get a sense for whether the person or people you're considering can wear all the required hats.

CHAPTER FIFTEEN

GETTING YOUR HOUSE IN ORDER

This final chapter is about being honest with yourself about when the advertising plan is not the problem. The biggest misconception I hear from marketing clients is a belief that they should always be doing more if they want better results. "I'm selling 10,000 widgets per month," they say (usually a male CEO). "Now tell me. *What more should I be doing?*" For some people (usually the male CEO type), better is always additive. If doing this is getting me there, hadn't I better double up on that to get me all the way?

What I don't tell my non-erotica clients, but what I will tell you, is that marketing is a lot like sex. More is *not* always better. Going harder, faster, freakier on advertising does *not* always improve the experience, let alone speed along the desired result. No amount of better marketing will make a book with a bad funnel experience sell. The funnel experience describes what prospective readers will see on their path to deciding whether to buy your book. If your book simply doesn't show well, don't waste money on advertising.

I see a lot of authors making excuses for themselves, particularly when it comes to reviews. Bad reviews are everyone else's fault but theirs. When they get a bad review, they go onto Facebook and cry about it to their friends, who are quick to assure them the people who issued them must be idiots or trolls. But this is career-limiting behavior. Get your Facebook friends to sympathize with you over things that don't impact your career, like the fact that the next season of *A Game of Thrones* isn't coming out for another sixteen months. Unless you are satisfied with the number of readers you have, don't let the group of people who already like your work tell you that it's just fine.

I guarantee you that if you don't have a rating of at least 4.5 stars, you are losing prospective readers who are on the fence about your book. I'm not saying all ratings are fair, or that a four-star rating is bad. I'm saying that the reasons why ratings exist is to signal quality. If you don't have top ratings, spend time fixing that. A better rating could double your conversion rate.

Other authors who made cost-saving decisions when they first put together their books want to turn to advertising to boost sales. Sometimes, better advice is to look candidly at your asset library and be honest with yourself about whether it's strong. If your cover's just okay, take the money you would have spent on advertising this month and have your cover redesigned instead. Hire a book marketing or blurb consultant to tell you what is and isn't working about your description.

It's the lipstick on a pig concept. You shouldn't be spending money dressing up ads designed to sell more copies of your book if your book has strikes against it that will make it much harder to sell. I would rather see you start advertising with better assets later than I would have you advertise an asset that can't perform. If your core assets need help, the time to fix them is now.

Finally, before you spend money, are you doing everything you can that is free? I won't be shy about telling you that I suck at running my own Facebook and Twitter pages. Chances are you already know smart things you could be doing better to improve your results. Sometimes, you have found the enemy and she is you.

GO FORTH AND SELL BOOKS!

The marketing world is ever-changing—the publishing world, too. Even as I wrote some of these chapters, I was aware that any of the rules, norms, and entities I referred to could easily turn on a dime. As I gain new insights, and as big things change, I'll revise this manuscript and publish new editions. To stay current on what's happening in the world of marketing erotic romance, visit www.marketingsteamyromance.com and join my newsletter to receive updates on my blog.

And you'll find more than updates on the website. A wealth of content that I didn't include will be discussed on that forum instead. Things that didn't make sense to dive into specifically, because they were out of scope or because they were nearly certain to change will be maintained on my far more flexible web site. You'll find reviews of more general marketing courses, summaries of marketing and craft books I like, and an index of specific niche advertisers, and a list of erotic romance publishers, to name a few.

CLICHÉS AND PLATITUDES

So, now we've reached the end. Here's where I'm supposed to give you a final pep talk—to tell you that you *can* do this and to send you on your eager way. Indeed, you *can* do this. But the power I hope I've instilled in sharing my insights is not a sense of blind optimism, but rather a better understanding of the rules of the game. The authors whose book sales would turn your eyes green with envy aren't the ones who are writing the best books. They're the ones who have the focus to understand what's important in the marketing game, and who have learned how to play it smart.

And not just smart, but tough. You're in the ring—now be a gladiator. Yes, that was a *Scandal* reference, and if you need extra motivation, buy a white designer bath robe and, when you sit down at your computer, channel your inner Olivia Pope. This business isn't for the faint of heart. Know only that a business is what this is and that you'll be more profitable, more recognized, *more read*, if you treat it like one.

AFTERWORD

I wouldn't be setting my own example as a marketer if I didn't do three things:

1. Ask you to take just a few minutes to give an honest review on the site of the retailer where you bought the book
2. Invite you to become a subscriber to the Marketing Steamy Romance website
3. Give you an invitation to check out my other books

In the very last pages, you'll find two previews. If you're looking for something sexy, fun and nostalgic, my novella, *The Art of Worship*, might be your speed:

Teenage virgin Reed Whitney stands to inherit a cache of lovemaking wisdom that has been passed down through generations. There's only one problem: the knowledge is shared directly from father to son. Sorely lacking in prowess, Reed is desperate to please his girlfriend, Aubrey. But can he survive the awkward embarrassment of instruction from his dad and learn the art of worship?

The second excerpt is for *Snapdragon*, my hot, dry-witted, and glamorous friends-with-benefits duet:

The rules are simple: unattached companionship, toe-curling sex and a clean break whenever it ends. Either one can say the single word that will break it off: Snapdragon.

Both are available in paperback and ebook. Head to kilbyblades.com to brows a list of retailers where my books are sold.

ACKNOWLEDGMENTS

Bex Dane is not, by profession, a marketer. She is nonetheless among the most disciplined marketers I've met. When I was a hot shot newbie who knew everything about general marketing but nothing about book marketing, Bex took me under her wing. Even as I chase down my deadline on submitting this book, she's cheering me on from the sidelines. Thank you. Thanks also to Marisa Shor of Cover Me Darling who hooked me up with this gorgeous cover. Check out her work. It's amazing.

The dozens of other authors who helped make this book a reality are many, most of who I don't know how to honor by name. Through Facebook groups and message boards, chat conversations and e-mail conversations, I learned from strangers who generously gave their best tips and warnings in the spirit of supporting other authors the community. Thank you all.

ABOUT KILBY BLADES

When not writing steamy romance under her pen name, Kilby Blades is the Chief Marketing Officer of a successful tech start-up. After earning her MBA from a top 3 U.S. program in 2005, she juggled a busy career leading digital media for a decorated New York marketing agency with raising two kids and moonlighting as a writer and editor.

Prior to launching her original fiction career, she was an award-winning travel essayist and non-fiction book writer, an adored fan fiction author, a successful ghostwriter and a well-syndicated blogger with columns on Huffington Post, Examiner.com and a leading entertainment blog.

Her debut novel, *Snapdragon*, was a Semi-Finalist in the 2017 Publisher's Weekly BookLife Prize For Fiction. She is a certified sommelier, an oenophile, a cinephile, and above all, a hopeless fic fiend.

Want to stay connected?
www.marketingsteamyromance.com
kilby@kilbyblades.com

THE ART OF WORSHIP: PREVIEW

CHAPTER 1

"Reed, may I see you in my study?"

My father's casual tone is displaced, as if he invites me into his study with regularity. Which he doesn't.

"I thought that since your mother was out, we might have a talk, just the two of us."

As we walk silently toward the east wing of the house, I wonder what this could be about. I'm eighteen, a senior in high school. My grades are excellent. I never stay out past curfew or get in trouble. And if he ever found the small stash of pot I keep in my underwear drawer, I doubt he'd care.

But there are some things my father takes seriously—like anything that happens in his study. And I'm curious to know why he's summoned me. It's a distinguished space. The hand-crafted wood shelves that stand from floor to ceiling hold first editions of classics and other rare books. The furniture has been passed down through generations, along with mementos from across the globe. A fire blazes brightly in a hearth nearly as tall as the two of us. An old phonograph playing Chopin crackles and whines.

Every time I'm here, I get the feeling that I am stepping into another century. I half expect the portraits of Whitney men that hang on the walls, to come alive. These men are more serious versions of my father and me—oceanic eyes stare down past haughty cheekbones. One day it will be my own son and great-grandson who stand in this room inspecting a portrait of me.

"Scotch?" he asks, closing the door needlessly before striding to his liquor trolley.

It places me on alert. He only likes us to drink together when he has something to get off his chest. The last time he called me in for a man-to-man was the night they gave me the Jeep. We'd gotten through a third of a bottle of Blue Label before he'd said his peace on the privilege of driving a car and the responsibilities that go along with it.

"Thank you," I accept, in a tone as cordial and controlled as his. For as much as I'm just a kid, I've been well-trained in the protocols of high-born men.

I take a seat on the leather chair that faces his direction just as he pulls out a well-aged Laphroaig. I study him, for clues, as he drops a single ice cube into each tumbler, pours us each two fingers of whiskey, and travels to join me in the chair opposite mine. He gives away nothing and, as usual, I don't know whether to resent his distance or to respect the hell out of his discipline. No teenage kid wants to admit to idolizing his dad, but in many ways, I do.

He settles in next to me, resting the bottle on the table in between us as he places one of the tumblers in my hand. I meet his eyes, and we raise our glasses in a silent toast, before turning our gazes to the fire. The whiskey tastes good and I make a mental note to raid his supply. The cheap stuff is fine for the flask I bring to school, but I wouldn't mind enjoying a nip or two of this in the privacy of my own room.

"You and Aubrey are close," he finally begins, after a few minutes.

Hmmm...he wants to talk about Aubrey. I don't give an answer because I can tell he doesn't expect one.

"Your mother seems to think you two are—*being intimate*—with each other."

Brilliant—now they're speculating on my sex life.

"Are you?"

I feel his eyes slide back to me. I keep my face neutral, my eyes on the fire.

"Yes, we're very close," I say calmly.

"But have you been intimate with one another?"

To anyone else, his voice would have sounded perfectly even, but I sense his slight annoyance. He doesn't like how good I've become at his subtle brand of insolence. The corner of my mouth quirks upwards in amusement as I look back over at him. I think about apples and trees and things that don't fall far from one another.

"Are you referring to the special way a man and a woman hug when they love one another?"

Yes, it's wicked of me, but he's asking for it. He's a doctor—can't he just come out and say S-E-X ?

"You underestimate me, Reed," he retorts evenly. "Even if you can't believe that I was your age once, at least give me credit for living closer to reality than the other parents in this town. Remember, I'm the one prescribing their kids birth control and helping them figure out what to do when they don't use it."

I want to tell him not to underestimate *me*, to give *me* credit for not being one of the incompetent brood I go to school with but I think the better of it. I distill my thoughts into a more diplomatic response.

"Don't worry, Dad. I know that the pill is over 97% effective if taken as directed. I know that condoms and abstinence are the only ways to reduce the risk of STDs, and that condoms must be applied properly—with the tip pulled up flat and empty—in order for them to work."

See how I threw in that shit about abstinence? It never hurts to keep your parents guessing.

"I know you know those things. I know you'll take measures to protect you and Aubrey and I hope you know that if anything unexpected happens you can trust your mother and me enough to come to us for help."

And I know it's true. My parents are decent people, and I've got it better than a lot of kids. They'd be pissed if I got Aubrey pregnant, but they wouldn't freak out, and I respect them for that.

Conceding, I say "I appreciate that...but, Dad...why are we here?"

He swirls his glass again, the remaining sliver of ice a mere shard floating in honey-colored liquid. I followed suit as he looks back toward the hearth, patiently waiting for him to reveal the purpose of our conversation.

"Have I ever told you how much your grandmother Eleanor disapproved of your mother?"

I shake my head and straighten in my seat a little. He almost never speaks of his parents, who were killed in a small plane crash years before I was born. I am surprised, and intrigued, that he speaks of them now and that any of it has to do with my mother. For years, I've been eager to know more about them.

"She wouldn't even give me her engagement ring to ask for your mother's hand. Even though Kate came from her own money, she came up with every excuse for why we shouldn't be together. She thought Kate was after our money, that she was pursuing other men simultaneously for *their* money, that she was sleeping with other men...she named every conceivable charge you could level against a woman trying to marry into a family like ours."

"Why she believed this about your mother was a different story, a misunderstanding I'll share with you at another time. But your grandfather, my father, never believed a word of it. He knew not only that your mother loved me, but that she was loyal, and would be a faithful wife. He knew I never had to worry about her straying from me because our love was real."

Preston turned back to look at me pointedly.

"He knew I could satisfy her every need."

Wait…what?

He can't mean —

When my father raises a confirming eyebrow, I can only gape in mortification.

Jesus, dad — *TMI!*

As he lets his subtext fully sink in, I am flushed with embarrassment.

"Son, you are here to receive a precious gift. It is one that my father bestowed upon me, and that his father bestowed upon him —one I will pass on to you now and expect that you give to your own sons when it is time."

What. The. Fuck?

"You are a Whitney, and were therefore born with certain natural—*endowments*—that predispose you to success with women. But, there is a beauty in sex which, if you could only grow to appreciate it—an art which, if you could only commit to learning it—will bring you and the women in your life such divine fulfillment as most mortals never know. It is the art of worship, Reed, and it has very little to do with sex."

His gaze is intense and I can barely breathe, let alone process my surprise that such a cache of Whitney family wisdom exists. My father is subtle most of the time, but when he isn't he can be quite intimidating. It doesn't help that he's hit the nail on the head about my need for some, erm…guidance. The truth is, I've been consumed with worry about pleasing Aubrey.

"So, I'll ask you again, son. Have you and Aubrey been intimate with one another?"

I shake my head in sheepish truth.

"But, you plan to be."

I nod.

"Very good…" he smiles, polishing off the rest of his glass, "…then, there's still time."

───

Ha! Want to hear Preston's advice? Head to www.kilbyblades.com/the-art-of-worship/ for links to where you can pick up the rest of the novella.

CHAPTER 1

"CAN YOU HAND ME MY diaper bag, Darbs? I don't think I can reach it."

Charlotte sat on the Chesterfield wearing nothing but Spanx and the frumpiest corset that Darby had ever seen. The pale pink garment looked like it was made of some sort of cotton material. It sported heavy utilitarian zippers, with a complex opening around the nipple that was designed to allow breast shield fixtures to fit through. An enormous yellow pump that she recognized as hospital grade sucked and wheezed rhythmically from where it sat, plugged in, on the floor. Darby could hear the faint sound of milk dripping into twin four ounce bottles that jutted out unnaturally from the contraption.

"Which one is it?" Darby set down her champagne.

She looked between the two stylish totes sitting near her feet.

"Not the Petunia Picklebottom—the Storsak."

Darby looked back down at the bags. "Am I supposed to know the difference?"

"It's the one that looks like a Longchamp," a heavily pregnant

Jodi interjected as she waddled in from the other room. "The Petunia Picklebottom is the one that looks like a messenger bag." She gave a pointed look to Charlotte before turning her chin toward Darby. "You've got to translate when you're dealing with this one. She has no idea what any of this shit means."

Darby handed Charlotte the correct bag just as Jodi put her hand on the arm of the sofa to steady herself before sinking down with a groan. She was only thirty-six weeks along, but she looked like she'd have given her first born away if it meant the second one would come sooner.

The sound of a toilet flushing got all three women's attention, their eyes registering sympathy as they turned toward the sound. Iris was past her first trimester but the morning sickness was more like all day sickness and it showed no signs of letting up.

"I remember that," Charlotte commiserated, sharing a look with Jodi before flipping the pump off with her toes. She handled the milk bottles carefully as she extricated them from the apparatus and screwed the lids on tight. Only when the bottles were safe and sealed on the end table did she begin to fully disentangle herself. Pumping breast milk was a complex operation—one of many badges of motherhood that Darby didn't envy.

"Next time, I'm adopting," Iris groused, looking wrung out as she walked back into the lounge area. Her up do was disheveled, her face was blotchy, and her eyes looked slightly dazed.

"I know it's hard." Charlotte cast Iris an empathetic glance. "But experiencing pregnancy is part of being a woman. It's a major rite of passage. This is God's work you're doing."

In order to stop an unfriendly retort from spilling from her mouth, Darby took a long gulp of champagne.

Jodi patted the seat next to her as she cast a worried glance at Darby. "We got you some more Canada Dry, sweetie," she said to Iris.

"Thanks." Iris sat down gingerly, taking a fresh hand towel from Charlotte's pile.

The small group of women had taken over the ladies' lounge next to the ballroom of a South Florida hotel, one posh enough to accommodate their needs. They'd brought hand towels for Charlotte, cool compresses for Jodi's swollen feet, ginger ale for Iris and two ice buckets full of champagne. They'd even brought a tray of canapés, but the smell of smoked salmon and caviar was what had set Iris off. Sounds from the wedding reception could be heard from far down the hall, but Darby and her friends were content to have their own little party right there.

Recognizing herself for what she was—the only fully-mobile member of her party—Darby had seen to the needs of her friends. She'd kept the champagne flowing—everyone except for Iris was drinking—and she was having a good time catching up.

As the lone singleton among her group of old friends, Darby was used to the baby talk. By then, she'd surrendered to the idea that debates about sleep training and attachment parenting would play into many conversations. She had learned to anticipate the way these rare reunions had her feeling out of place.

When her friends had begun to marry, Darby hadn't minded admiring engagement rings with FL clarity, or bearing the mild insult of repeated insistence that life was so much better in the suburbs, and she didn't mind cooing over videos of fat-cheeked infants now. She'd quieted her judgments about how quickly so many of her friends had given up promising careers, and learned to ignore the disinterest in their expressions when she began to talk about hers. But even Darby had her limit. Dear God, if she had to endure one more heated debate about a Montessori vs. Waldorf school, someone was going to end up with a Sophie Giraffe shoved up her ass.

"What in the ever-loving fuck is this?"

Darby had just set down a fresh glass of champagne for Charlotte when she saw the small white box that had appeared on the end table next to the milk.

"What?" Charlotte didn't look from where her attention was

focused—on rummaging through her diaper bag—but Darby picked up the box. She read from it aloud.

"Milkscreen for breastfeeding. Detects alcohol in breast milk?"

She looked around the room in alarm.

Charlotte finally looked up. "If you've had too much to drink, you do a pump and dump. We owe it to our children to be responsible."

"Girls," Darby said matter-of-factly. "You know when our own moms were pregnant and nursing, they drank and smoked, right? Like, a lot."

"It was the seventies," Jodi laughed cheekily, taking a sip of her champagne. "Our moms did a lot of stuff."

Charlotte shot Jodi withering glare, looking between Jodi's protruding stomach and her glass.

Jodi pinned her with an unrepentant look. "What? I'm at the end of my third trimester."

"This product is obviously designed to capitalize on parents' fears." Darby ignored their exchange. "They've done studies on this. In France, Australia, and other cultures where moms drink during pregnancy and breastfeeding, light drinking shows very few effects."

Charlotte cast her a pitying look. "You'll understand when you're a mother, Darby."

And there it was. She'd been waiting for it. Iris and Jodi never pressured her about her status, but Charlotte was always digging in.

"What makes you think I want to be a mother?"

She finally set the box down and picked her champagne back up.

"Don't you?" Charlotte was genuinely shocked.

Darby sat back down in her seat. "Frankly, no."

And miss out on all this awesomeness?

"Most women do," Charlotte argued.

Ever the scientist, Darby wanted proof. "What are you basing that on?"

"History," Charlotte insisted. "Even in cultures in which monogamy isn't valued, childbearing is."

"History's been pretty shitty to women," Darby said evenly, taking a sip of her drink. "Forced marriages, non-consensual sex between husbands and wives…that's still going on in a lot of places."

"So just because women didn't always have children on their own terms…are you saying that having children wouldn't have been their choice?"

"Not for some of them." Charlotte raised skeptical eyebrows, but Darby stood her ground. "Don't look at me like that. We've evolved. We've stopped pressuring gay people into straight, childbearing marriages. We have access to birth control. We get to choose. And a lot of us don't choose that."

"Alright…" Charlotte nearly pouted. "Tell me you at least want to get married. I think you could be really happy with the right guy."

Charlotte, who had the exact life that she had always envisioned for herself, was practically oozing what she felt was justified concern for her old friend.

"Oh my God, Char. Leave the woman alone!" Jodi finally interjected, her playful wit disarming any tension.

She turned to Darby. "Nobody's judging you, Darbs. And if we were, we wouldn't have a right to." Jodi paused to look briefly and pointedly at Charlotte. "We sit at home on our fat asses every night, watching Netflix and folding laundry, and having bad sex every once in a blue moon with stretched out post-baby vag."

Iris chuckled a bit and shared an affirming look with Jodi. "It's like throwing a hot dog down a hallway."

Jodi nodded her agreement. "Meanwhile, Darby still looks young and gorgeous, fucks whoever she wants, and has tight pussy sex."

They all laughed at that, all irritation forgotten. Darby rarely saw these women, and it felt good to get together like this. Back home in Chicago, she didn't have many friends. But she knew things would be different if she had to take them in larger doses. They'd each grown into new people since high school and their differences as adults were hard to ignore.

"You know I'm the same age as all of you, right?"

"You don't look it," Charlotte admitted ruefully. "Your face has the youthful glow of someone who's actually getting sleep."

Mention of sleep led to a conversation about how many hours of cartoons it was okay to let your kids watch first thing in the morning when you wanted a few more winks. When it devolved into a debate over which show did a better job of addressing sibling rivalry—Daniel Tiger or Peppa Pig—Darby took that as her cue to leave.

After she had slipped out of the ladies' lounge, she dismissed the idea of returning to the wedding reception, content instead to retreat outdoors. She took pleasure in the warm air on the elegant marble patio and leaned against one of the cool walls encircling the grand ballroom. Darby liked old hotels, and beaches, and she enjoyed the blanket of stars twinkling brighter than they ever did in the city.

She had missed the sounds of waves hitting the shore and luxuriated in the way that the ocean breeze gently stirred the ends of her long dark auburn hair and tickled her lips. It reminded her of similar evenings spent in the one place she'd always been happy—her family's house on Lake Geneva.

"You look like you're having about as much fun as I am."

A smooth masculine voice broke Darby from her thoughts. She let her gaze drift away from the animated party going on inside. Even in low light, she could see that the man who'd appeared next to her was uniquely handsome, his full lips and strong jaw betraying an otherwise slender, heart-shaped face. His nose was uncommonly wide toward the middle, as if it had been broken at some point, but it flattered him.point, but it flattered him.

"Oh, much, much more…" Darby teased.

Something about the sarcasm in his voice compelled her to answer more acerbically than she normally would to a total stranger.

"What gave me away?" She angled herself toward him.

Taking a better look, she saw that he was clean-shaven and tall with a swimmer's build, a buzz cut that hinted at nearly-black hair. His tanned skin offset some of the most striking dark blue eyes she'd ever seen.

"Staying as far away as physically possible from the wedding party is usually a clue."

A smile hinted at the corner of his mouth. The combination of full lips and slight laugh lines that would surely improve with age elevated his status from striking to outright sexy. The world was full of beautiful men, but it wasn't every day she came face to face with one this good-looking.

"So I guess that's what you're doing out here?"

He nodded slightly, as if to admit he was just as guilty. Darby took a hearty swig of her champagne and for a moment they both looked back toward the party.

"Are you like this at all weddings or is there something about this one in particular?"

His question drew her gaze back to his, and she was glad to have an excuse to look at him again.

"All weddings. Though, I knew it was time to get some air when my friend started needling me about when I was going to meet a guy, buy a house with a white picket fence, and have two point five kids."

He nodded in understanding. "I've been hassled about that before. Getting some air was the right call."

"She pulls the same shit on me every time," Darby complained lightly. "I should have just said I had a boyfriend, or worn a decoy engagement ring. It would be a good excuse to buy myself a diamond."

The man weaved his head and let hesitation paint his features. "Yeah, but then you'd have to stage a fake wedding, dig up a fake fiancé, hire an actor to officiate…"

She feigned regret. "Yeah, I guess you're right."

They both chuckled.

"Well, if it's any consolation, I was just groped."

She raised her eyebrows. "Groped?"

"By a married woman, no less. She spent the first two courses with her hand on my knee, then my thigh, then…"

Her mouth fell open. He nodded in grave confirmation. "And her husband was sitting right there. I feel so…violated." His eyes twinkled as she laughed.

"You can't go back in there. You know that, right?"

"Well, if I can't, neither can you."

Interesting.

"Isn't it rude to leave before the cake is cut?" Her protest was halfhearted.

"Maybe we could go for a walk."

Five minutes later, they were descending to the beach via ancient stone steps that were carved into the cliff walls. It was dark. The steps were wide and steep and without a railing. Slight vertigo, plus the fact that she was wearing tall heels, had given Darby a moment of pause. But the stranger beside her gallantly allowed her to remain on the inside while offering a steady hand.

A walk on the beach was the perfect antidote to a lackluster night. The humidity of south Florida made the air balmy, and the breeze coming off of the ocean put Darby even more at ease. As they floated down in companionable silence, the sound of their steps was muffled by the rushing water.

She didn't know why she hadn't thought of this herself. She was used to seeing water every day, but Lake Michigan did not compare to the ocean. Before they had left the party to wander down the beach, her new friend had slipped back inside the ballroom just long enough to procure an unopened bottle of champagne and two flutes. He now opened the bottle and poured her a glass, just moments after they reached the beach and took off their shoes. He did it with practiced ease and raised his glass in a brief, silent toast, as if champagne walks on the beach with women he'd just met were something he did every day. As they began walking toward the water, it occurred to Darby that she knew nothing about the handsome stranger next to her.

"So do you have a name?"

"Michael Blaine, 31. Born and raised in Chicago. Architect with Dewey and Rowe. I have a twin sister, Bex, and a niece, Ella. When I'm not at work, which isn't very often, I spend my time with them."

His voice was calm and honest.

"You?"

"Darby Christensen, 32. Also from Chicago. Psychiatrist at Northwestern Memorial. No siblings, but I do have a hermit crab named Consuela. My only other family is my dad, but I don't see very much of him."

She watched him attentively, wondering whether he would make the connection to Frank Christensen like so many others did, whether he would ask about her father, about what it was like to be a controversial senator's daughter.

"Are you a friend of the bride or the groom?" he inquired instead.

"Benji and I went to boarding school together. I've known him since the sixth grade."

Recognition dawned on Michael's face, and he stopped walking to turn toward her.

"Wait, was there another Darby in your class, or are you *the* Darby?"

His question was a formality—Darby wasn't a common name.

"I'm guessing I'm *the Darby*."

Michael took a sip of champagne, the narrow flute doing little to hide his knowing smile.

"I take it Ben's mentioned me before?" she asked.

"Once or twice." He said it in a way that guaranteed he was understating the truth. "All good things."

Darby shook her head.

"Uh-uh. You gotta give me more than that."

His smile hadn't disappeared, only softened.

"I was his roommate all four years at Tufts."

"Wait, you're Mickey Blue Eyes?"

Memories flooded back to her as he let out a short laugh.

"I forgot anyone ever called me that."

Darby wasn't about to let him off the hook so easily. "He always talked about how women fell all over you. I remember stories about girls leaving their underwear on your door and getting into catfights over you."

"That's an exaggeration." But his protest sounded weak.

"Girls breaking into your room to wait for you, naked, in bed was an exaggeration?"

He cast his shaking head down, smiling a bit at that.

"That only happened twice."

She laughed openly.

"Some of them were Ben's admirers," Michael insisted charitably.

"Uh-huh." Darby found his modesty endearing.

"I always thought he sounded a little jealous of you…" she mused aloud. *And now I can see why*, she thought to herself.

"I don't know about that." Michael said, still being quite modest. "Besides, he was too busy pining over you to be jealous of me. You have to know it took him a long time to get over you. Like, years."

Darby's respondent smile was bittersweet.

"He was my first love," she admitted, "the first boy I ever kissed, the first boy I ever…"

Michael smiled kindly. By then they'd reached the water's

edge. He freed one hand to place it on the small of her back, and guided her to the left, his small gesture saving her from having to say any more. He walked them along the shoreline, all the way down the beach. The moon shone brightly above them.

"My first time was with a professor..." he volunteered, perhaps compelled to disclose something personal about himself. "It was junior year of college —"

"But I thought —"

"That's exactly what I wanted them to think. I put on a good show of confidence back then, but I was actually pretty shy."

"So who was the professor?"

"She taught French Lit. Her name was Genevieve, but I called her Gigi."

She liked the wistfulness she heard in his voice as he recounted the tale.

"She asked me to be her TA the semester after I'd taken her class. We were grading midterms one holiday weekend — at her house, of course. The campus buildings were closed, and we had thirty term papers spread out all over her dining room table. We were debating the significance of one of the final lines of *Candide*, which roughly translates to 'we must cultivate our own garden' —"

"Il faut cultiver notre jardin," Darby translated. Her well-honed accent earned her a smile.

"The debate got heated — in a good way — and the next thing I knew, I was spread out all over her dining room table."

"Sounds hot." She shifted her gaze to him.

The moon was bright enough to see his face clearly, and his eyes masked nothing.

"It was."

"So how long did it last?"

He looked out at the water for a second before swinging his gaze back to her. When he stopped walking, she did the same.

"Long enough for her to give me the education every inexperienced teenage boy wants from a very experienced woman."

CHAPTER 2

DARBY AND MICHAEL SETTLED INTO a secluded cabana nestled in a grove of palm trees set far back from the water. From where they reclined, angled toward one-another on terry-topped cushions, they had a view of the moonlit water and clear night skies. Conversation was easy, as if they'd known one-another for years instead of merely knowing *about* one-another for years.

As they meandered from topic to topic, the things that Ben had told her about him came back to mind. Michael had rowed crew. He was a math prodigy. He had received some sort of important service award from The White House. As he opened up about his life, the things he said corroborated her resurfacing memories. Talking about their lives in Chicago also revealed new things. He was deeply involved in charitable work and tried to attend as many of the city's summer food and music festivals as he could.

He also ran along the same stretch of Lake Shore Drive that she did when the weather was nice. Darby could envision the run along the lakefront path clearly. She imagined his exact running wardrobe, right down to the Asics sneakers on his feet to the pristine white ear buds attached to his phone. She became somewhat distracted thinking about what he would look like wearing nothing but his Under Armour, his torso twisting to and fro as his leg muscles worked to propel him forward, his upper body bare and his shirt tucked into his shorts, revealing a sheen of sweat.

"So, no girlfriend, huh?"

He shook his head. "No girlfriend, no wife, no ex-wife. No boyfriend."

Given her current aversion to dating, it shouldn't have mattered to her whether Michael had a girlfriend. But Darby felt relieved. She didn't like to keep dubious company. And just because he wasn't wearing a ring didn't mean he was available.

"The seventy-hour work week's pretty much killed my chance at a normal love life," he admitted a moment later.

"Amen to that." His words rang so true that she could have been the one saying them. She shot him an empathetic look. "So what do you do…for company?"

It was the first time she saw him hesitate. She lifted her hands in a peaceful gesture. "I don't mean to pry. Really, I'm asking because I could use some advice myself."

"Me counseling you would be like the blind leading the blind. You could probably give me some pointers."

She nearly snorted. "Don't take advice from me. I'm days away from paying for it."

"And here I thought you were a nice girl," he kidded.

"Come on, Michael, we both know nice girls finish last."

He cocked his head to the left and narrowed his eyes in disbelief.

"You mean to tell me the good doctor doesn't get what she wants? Somehow I find that hard to believe."

"I can assure you, the woman-of-fortune-and–fame fantasy is much sexier than the reality."

"So's the one about the most eligible bachelor."

"Touché." She reached to smooth her hair, which the quickening breeze had blown across her face. "So what do you want that you can't have?"

"Companionship." He said it simply, as if the answer were quite obvious.

Something in the way he said it made her quell her temptation to dismiss the sentiment, however improbable it sounded.

"I'll bet you could find that if you wanted it. You recruited me easily enough."

"You want the truth?"

"I always want the truth."

Trepidation crossed his face. He took a breath before he spoke again.

"The truth is, I like you. I think you're the kind of girl I'd like to have dinner with and take to social functions. I think we'd have more good conversation, some fun times, and sizzling hot sex."

He paused long enough to measure her reaction. In the dark, he wouldn't have been able to see the goosebumps that prickled her flesh.

"But I don't need to start something with you to know how it'll end. Experience has taught me that women are biologically incapable of having unattached relationships. Since I'm too busy for the kind of commitment they want, I go without. I'd rather do that than lead them on."

Darby let out a measured breath. "Wow, that was…" *presumptuous*, she wanted to say. Though he delivered them gently, his words still cut.

"I know my share of women who are obsessed with getting a man to commit," she returned in the same tone. "And I respect you for not being the guy that leads that kind of woman on."

"But?" he smiled, sensing an unfavorable reaction.

"But your broad categorization of women is short-sighted." *And borderline sexist*. She bit her tongue again.

"If you think there aren't plenty of single women who want to stay that way, you are mistaken. My parents' marriage was a disaster, and the idea of emulating that repulses me. Despite all you've heard about biological clocks and maternal instincts, not all women have them. I have a career I love that has me working just as many hours as you do, probably more. The last thing I need is to come home after a hard day to somebody who is biologically incapable of not needing his ego stroked."

She didn't let on how much she was enjoying watching the widening of his eyes, the subtle slacking of his jaw. "And because I can't find a man who wants nothing more than to give me four toe curling orgasms twice a week and then get the hell out of my house…"

She saw the bob of his Adam's apple and was dying to know what other reactions she may have caused.

"Do you honestly expect me to believe that you can't find a guy who only wants to have sex with you?"

His voice was so low that it wiped out any doubt that the attraction was mutual.

"I expect you to believe girls like me have only two options: one-night stands and Romeos. I don't do one-night stands because the world is full of psychopaths who like doing bad things to pretty girls. And I stay away from Romeos because I find it insulting to watch someone go through the pomp and circumstance of "dating" me because he thinks that's what it'll take for me to sleep with him."

By the time she finished, she noted a change in his expression and she wondered whether her words had triggered something. Men could be fragile, especially the better looking ones.

"So, paint me a picture of someone who's different."

Her body hummed with the awareness of how quickly their conversation was leaving the realm of the hypothetical. The ocean breeze was light but the air between them was heavy.

"How would that someone come into your life?" he implored.

"It's complicated."

And it was. For Darby, there could be no innocent flirtations, no absent minded affairs, no tawdry trysts. Her father was a public figure, and she had her own respectable career to protect. She wasn't like every other woman her age who could take to Tinder every time she wanted a good time.

"I like complex things."

His breath near her ear made her tingle, and she had to concentrate to calm her voice lest it betray her emotions.

"He couldn't be a complete stranger. I'd have to meet him someplace safe and know that I could trust him." Saying it felt strange. As if she were creating a different persona. As if she were pretending some alternative could exist. "And there'd have to be a real attraction," she added.

"What else?"

"He'd respect me enough to be honest about our arrangement

and respect himself enough to be mature, conscientious, and discreet about the whole thing." She took a shaky breath. "And I, uh…wasn't kidding about the orgasms, either. They need to be toe-curling and there'd need to be at least four, every time we…"

He closed his eyes for a moment too long for it to be a blink. Darby wondered what he was imagining.

"What about you?" she said finally. "If you could find a woman who was different, how would things be?"

He took his time to answer, his eyes focused toward the water. Before he did, he turned back to her with a look of halting intensity. She sensed that he wanted to be completely honest though his deep blue eyes reserved an ocean of secrets. It only made him more intriguing. As a psychiatrist it was her job to read people, but she couldn't read him fully.

"I want a woman who doesn't confuse me loving her company with me being in love with her. She has to know that whatever we have today may not be there tomorrow, not because I'm heartless or distant or incapable of intimacy—but because right now, I choose my career, and my love isn't in play—only my companionship.

"I need a woman who's prepared for the fact that what we share won't feel transactional. It will feel intimate and intense, because I only spend time with women I genuinely like and because I take pride in doing things well. She needs to know that me showing her respect and treating her like a lady and making her feel worshipped has nothing to do with her being more special to me than a good friend and everything to do with my idea of how a woman deserves to be treated."

He put down his empty champagne flute, placing it absently on the cushion next to him so that he could turn his body toward her.

"She'd have to understand that it's never more than meets the eye—and that each of us is responsible to the other to break things off the second things get too complicated. And she has to be prepared for what's inevitable. Because the end will come,

Darby. Even if it doesn't get complicated, I'll make partner one day, or get transferred halfway around the world, or maybe even go to work for another firm. And my job comes first. It just...does."

She gazed over at him, her face mostly neutral as she listened without judgment. She could never help vacillating between regular-girl Darby and Dr. Darby, clinically-trained psychiatrist, deconstructor of everyone's problems. That line, no matter how often she tried to draw it, was made of disappearing ink.

"I think I understand."

He still looked cautious.

"You're honest with the women you date, but they don't act on what you say—they act on how you make them feel. You said that being with you feels intimate and intense. A woman who believes that a man has intense feelings for her has been programmed to believe that he'll initially resist commitment but that commitment is inevitable if the feelings are real. For them, the feelings and the commitment are mutually exclusive. But for you..."

"They're not."

"Which makes you the love 'em and leave 'em jerk who breaks their heart."

"Pretty much," he let out a humorless laugh.

She looked out at the ocean pensively but sensed him looking at her. It was another minute before she spoke.

"There was this guy, Dave," she began, still looking out toward the horizon. "We hung out one summer when I was interning in Manhattan. He was a real party guy—could get you into the VIP room at any club, or into the hottest parties in the Hamptons, could get you any drug. He was like the king of New York, and he made me feel like the queen."

"It started to feel like a relationship. He took me everywhere with him, showed me off to his friends...I even spent a bunch of time at his parents' place. They had this great house in Bergen County, and whenever he'd throw parties there, I'd crash. His mom even served me bagels for breakfast every morning. I took it as my cue to consider something serious."

"Were you in love with him?" Michael asked. She shook her head.

"He was a lot of fun. And the sex was good…like, really good," she said candidly. "I knew dating him for real would have been a disaster. But I still pursued him. It didn't matter that I was smart and independent and didn't subscribe to all the gender role bullshit—not consciously at least. I hated myself for chasing a guy I didn't even really want, but that backwards idea that getting a guy to commit is the ultimate goal was just too ingrained."

"So what happened?"

"I ruined it. By trying to turn it into something it wasn't. I ruined something really good."

"So you're not that kind of girl anymore?" he asked.

She shook her head. "I kind of hate that girl now," she admitted. "That 'first comes love, then comes marriage mentality' is toxic. The best relationships define themselves."

Michael was quick to echo her thoughts.

"You can't have it all. That's the biggest lie we tell ourselves. We act like it's achievable to have a great career, a happy family, and to find a soul mate who fulfills your every need. But that's the exception, not the rule. I can't be a dedicated architect, a doting partner, a loving father, a great brother, and a great uncle…so I've decided what I want, and what I can be good at, and I'll let the other chips fall where they may."

They held hands all the way back up the beach, feet sinking into the sand as the foamy surf lapped at their ankles. Words seemed unnecessary—perhaps enough had been said that night —but she was still disappointed to see the evening come to an end. The look he had given her when he had taken her hand hadn't been gentlemanly. His small touches and glances were magnetic, and she thought about what it would be like to see him again.

When they separated at the steps to brush off sandy feet and put their shoes back on, Darby almost spoke, convinced she should say something before she lost her nerve. Instead, his arm came around her shoulders, the other sweeping her up behind her knees. She drew a breath as she felt him start to carry her up the steps.

"You didn't think I was going to let you walk up a hundred steps in four-inch heels, did you?"

She felt the words vibrate as they formed in his chest, felt the solidity of his body beneath her. With her nose so close to his neck she could smell his skin, could easily inhale more of him. His fragrance was as complex as everything else about him. She wrapped her own arms around him, and leaned her head against his shoulder. Strong arms hadn't held her in a very long time.

They reached the top far too quickly and she was sorry when he gently set her down. Before they untangled themselves from each other's arms, he leaned in for a soft but thorough kiss. His thumbs caressed her cheeks as his tongue massaged hers with such expertise that she knew instantly that he'd be incredible at certain other things.

"What if I promised you five?" He pulled away only long enough to ask the question and fix her with a hawkish gaze before leaning in for seconds. "Would you see me if I promised you five?" He asked again only after he'd gently devoured her mouth once more.

"Lofty goal, Don't you think?" she murmured against his chin, not waiting for an answer before capturing his lips once again.

"I'm an overachiever," he said darkly as he pulled back.

"Six?" He nipped at her neck.

She might have laughed at his bravado if kissing him hadn't felt so good, and had his voice held any of the humor that should have accompanied such a ridiculous dare, yet his voice held no mirth.

The idea was ludicrous—six orgasms? Even the four she'd

mentioned had been an exaggeration. Still, a stab of anticipatory pleasure tingled up her spine as she realized this talented man might just deliver.

"This ends at sunrise," she managed, still out of breath as she pulled away long enough to say the words.

"I thought you didn't do one-night stands."

"It's not a one-night stand. It's an interview."

———

Want more? Head to www.kilbyblades.com/snapdragon

ALSO BY KILBY BLADES

Novels

Snapdragon (Love Conquers None: Part I of II)
Chrysalis (Love Conquers None: Part II of II)
The Secret Ingredient (Coming in 2018)

Novella

The Art of Worship

www.ingramcontent.com/pod-product-compliance
Lightning Source LLC
Chambersburg PA
CBHW070931210326
41520CB00021B/6884